HERALDRY
& REGALIA OF WAR

BEEKMAN HOUSE, NEW YORK

·M·LENZ·

Zeichnet·die·Sechste
Kriegsanleihe

HERALDRY
& REGALIA OF WAR

BEEKMAN HOUSE, NEW YORK

Introduction

The heraldry of war—the vivid, colourful display of uniforms, medals, badges and banners—has always been a heavy inducement to men to take up arms. But their main function is neither to confer glamour on their wearers, nor are they for mere empty display. There is, in the most sophisticated of men, something of the primitive. Our ancestors went into battle wearing war-paint, and with shields and weapons elaborately decorated: all part of the ritual whose purpose was to demonstrate the unity of the tribe. In the same way, modern man, whether in the thick of battle or in one of those situations of complete isolation that occur so frequently in modern war—deep in the bowels of a warship in action, in a trench under shellfire, or in the cockpit of an aeroplane with enemy aircraft in sight—needs a sense of identity with country and comrades. It is this sense of identity that the heraldry of war provides.

The cross section of uniforms, medals and insignia contained in this book can, then, be regarded as something more than a collection of colourful devices and complex diagrams. They provide a link between the purely functional need for immediate identification and the inborn need of man to dress himself for the occasion. A selection of the propaganda of the World Wars is also included, to illustrate the special rôle of the heraldry and regalia of war in uniting a whole nation in a common cause.

Edited by Bernard Fitzsimons

Phoebus, London.

This edition © BPC Publishing Ltd.
1973

First published in Purnell's History of
the World Wars

First published in this form 1973

ISBN 0 517 130866

Printed in Belgium - H. Proost & Cie p.v.b.a. Turnhout - Belgium

Contents

THE HERALDRY OF WAR
MEDALS INSIGNIA BADGES

All military heraldry is the perpetuation, for traditional reasons, of medals, insignia, uniforms, and flags that originally had a functional purpose. Sometimes the functional purpose has survived along side the tradition. New functional needs give rise to new devices which in their turn pass into tradition. Medals and orders have a long history, but it was not until the 18th Century that they began to be distributed to soldiers in the way that we now know. The original functional purpose of awarding medals was twofold. As an incentive to good service and courageous conduct medals have rarely been bettered, and the mystique that surrounds the highest awards for gallantry sheds glamour on their holders even in this anti-hero age. But lesser medals had an equally important purpose. The award of medals for campaign service ensured that a commander inspecting a regiment could decide almost at a glance how much experience, and of what kind, that regiment had. Hence medals, both for service and for courage, have proliferated, and here we show a cross-section of the medals of the World Wars.

The functional importance of naval flags has always outweighed their decorative value. Originally flag signals had been the only method of communicating between two ships at sea, and in spite of the advent of wireless they were still used as the main means of communication in the First World War. That they were unable to fulfil this rôle satisfactorily was shown both at Dogger Bank and at Jutland, but nonetheless the flags and naval insignia we illustrate this week played an important part in the war.

Aircraft markings and insignia constitute a huge and complicated subject, and we do not claim to have covered it comprehensively. It became apparent early in the war that aircraft required identifying marks, both to distinguish friend from foe in the air, and to prevent ground troops shooting at their own aircraft. Aircraft, unlike ground troops, were not bound by the need to camouflage themselves, so that where it was permitted colourful and eccentric individual markings were adopted, as well as national and unit insignia. Both are illustrated

Unlike medals, unit and formation badges are still more concerned with function than with morale or mystique. Designed at once to enlighten friend and baffle foe, unit markings of formations over the size of a battalion represent a proliferation of ingenious designs, ranging from straightforward initials through keys, stars, horseshoes, animals, to puns on the commander's name. Originally the *esprit de corps* of a British formation was based on its local identity, Scottish, west country, and so on. But as the war took its toll and units became more and more mixed, the badges replaced the territory of origin as the point of identity. Men became immensely proud of their unit sign. The BEF in France was the largest force that Britain has ever deployed in one theatre for as long as four years, and in the close proximity of the Western Front men came to know each formation well, and each took on a distinct character, a character that was partly determined by the badge of each formation. In the following pages we offer examples of the many unit signs of the wars

DEVELOPMENT OF THE FIGHTING MAN

100 AD

1150-1200

1640

1740

The need for uniform as we know it today arose with the development of standing armies of professional soldiers. For many years, potentates who raised armies for national or personal service had dressed their men in distinguishing uniforms or colours; but, in general, armies consisted of individuals who simply slung their weapons over their everyday dress. Even *they* found the need to distinguish friend from foe, and took to wearing 'field signs'—an armband or other distinctive device on their clothes, or a hat decoration—a practice which lasted until the English Civil War in the 1640s.

The history of uniform is bound up with the fascinating story of arms and armour. The Roman army, which developed its own technique of close-quarter disciplined fighting, evolved a standardised style of armour protection for the legionaries: helmet, body and shoulder armour, and a semi-cylindrical shield. Disciplined, armoured infantry tactics did not vanish with the collapse of the Roman Empire; the Danes, Norsemen, and English 'house carls' were formidable exponents of the battleaxe and shield wall. But their day ended with the Norman development of the armoured knight; and this began a new era in the history of armour, extending protection to the whole of the body—and eventually to the horse—to make the knight as formidable a juggernaut as possible. Yet the heavily-armoured knight was defenceless with the advent of infantry firepower, first with the longbow and later with the arquebus and early matchlock musket.

Armour for the infantry in the form of helmet and breastplate lingered on into the 17th Century and was worn by pikemen, who were important to infantry formations until the widespread adoption of the better flintlock musket with its ring bayonet. This weapon appeared when armies were assuming a more professional status; and few were more efficient than the Prussian army machine perfected by Frederick the Great.

Armoured protection was therefore replaced by colourful uniforms—and few armies in history have been more gorgeously attired than those of Napoleon's *Grand Armée*. It set so potent a tradition that it was imitated in the French uniforms of 1914.

The First World War rammed home what had been discovered in the Boer War: the need for a drab, functional uniform—which was even more necessary in the Second World War and after. Yet even today the lure of the uniform lives on in ceremonial.

1814

1914

1941

1968

Deidre Amsden

7

FROM FREDERICK THE GREAT TO WELLINGTON: 1740-1815

△ Prussian infantryman. He belonged to an army which earned the reputation of having the harshest discipline in the world. Drilled to fear his own superiors more than any enemy, he was liable to savage peacetime punishments, and in battle NCOs stood behind the line with drawn swords, waiting to run through any soldier who turned his back on the enemy. The Prussian uniform was severe but practical—although the pigtail was still an essential embellishment. Frederick's infantry was rock-hard on the battlefield, backed up by a small but superbly-led cavalry force; his army enabled him to seize Silesia, the richest province in the Habsburg domains, and to hold it against all comers in the Seven Years War

▷ British infantry in the field, 1815. Much had been learned by the British army since the days of Frederick the Great. By this time, the shako had replaced the tricorn hat, and the pigtail had vanished— although the pipeclayed crossbelts remained for many years. Yet in many ways the drill was as severe as Frederick's, for the British 'thin red line' owed its devastating battlefield success to a methodical fire-drill which had to be learned until it was automatic. It earned undying dividends at Waterloo and again 40 years later in the Crimea

Far left: Soldiers of the Confederate States of America. *Left to right:* captain (infantry), colonel (artillery), general, sergeant (cavalry), cavalry trooper in cape, infantryman in cape, infantryman, and corporal (artillery). The uniforms were a standard grey, the various arms being distinguished by different colours — the infantry a darker grey, the artillery red, and the cavalry yellow.

Left: Their rivals — soldiers of the US Army, 1864. *Left to right:* officer in greatcoat (mounted), infantry corporal, lieutenant-colonel, infantry sergeant, infantryman, infantryman in cape, and infantry officer in field uniform. The uniform is standard, rank being shown by shoulder and arm badges.

Right: A sergeant of the Duke of Cornwall's Light Infantry in parade uniform, 1914

Right centre: An Imperial German infantryman of the same date in marching order, with rifle, pack, canteen, and *pickelhaube* helmet

Far right: A British infantryman of 1916, with wire cutters, grenade, gas mask, and steel helmet

Below: A parade of the 68th Durham Light Infantry in 1864. The uniform displays little change from that of the Crimean War, the change being in the weapons. By 1860 the breech-loading rifle was in general service in the British army. The shakos are similar to those of 1815

National Army Museum

National Army Museum

Julian Allen

National Army Museum

11

Headgear in Evolution

1. Helmet of the mid-11th Century; variants were worn by both Normans and English at Hastings, by mounted knights and 'house-carls'
2. An Italian close helmet of the early 17th Century, with contours designed to deflect blows from any direction
3. Cutting down the weight: Cromwellian 'lobster-tail' helmet of 1640
4. This particular shako was proposed for

British regiments raised after 1815. It was not, however, adopted
5. Prussian cuirassier officer's helmet, 1842; a *pickelhaube* with neck protection, a feature which was to produce the 'coal-scuttle' design
6. This officer's helmet of the Norfolk Regiment, worn between 1871 and 1914, resembles the *pickelhaube* except for its cloth covering
7. This type of *képi* was worn by privates of

Saxon infantry regiments in the Imperial German army about 1900

8. The 1st Prussian Foot Guards wore this type of hat in 1900. Of 18th Century vintage, the type was kept on for ceremonial reasons

9. In the Austro-Hungarian army, the Polish Legion wore the *czapka* up to 1915

10. Uhlan (lancer) regiments of the German army in 1914 wore this style of helmet

11. The head-dress of the Royal Horse Artillery, known as a busby

12. This Japanese cap of the First World War reflects the modernising influence of Western technology on the Japanese forces

13. This type of *pickelhaube* was worn by German officers between 1891 and 1914

14. The *pickelhaube* worn by German infantrymen was basically the same as the previous

one, with a cloth cover for camouflage. The spike was detachable

15. A rare example of the French *poilu*'s helmet: the addition of a 'polack' face visor (c. 1916)

16. The British helmet of the First World War

17. The German helmet of the First World War; it gave protection to the side and back of the neck. Compared with its Second World War equivalent, it was wider and deeper

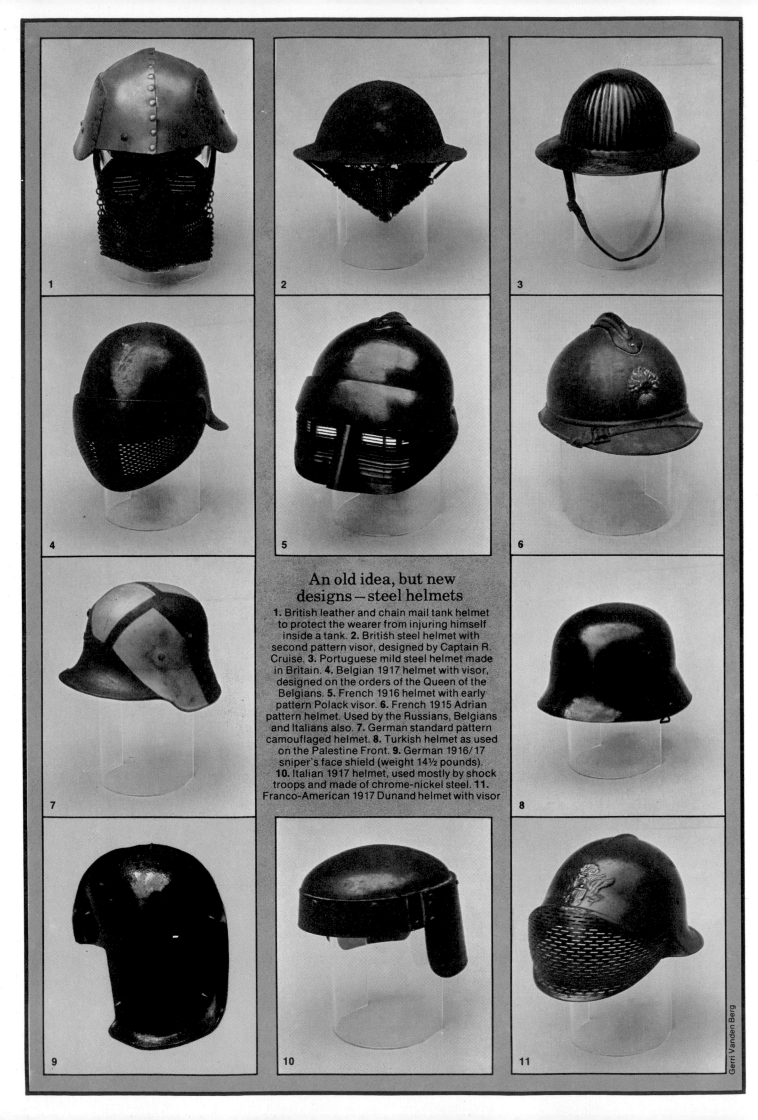

An old idea, but new designs — steel helmets

1. British leather and chain mail tank helmet to protect the wearer from injuring himself inside a tank. **2.** British steel helmet with second pattern visor, designed by Captain R. Cruise. **3.** Portuguese mild steel helmet made in Britain. **4.** Belgian 1917 helmet with visor, designed on the orders of the Queen of the Belgians. **5.** French 1916 helmet with early pattern Polack visor. **6.** French 1915 Adrian pattern helmet. Used by the Russians, Belgians and Italians also. **7.** German standard pattern camouflaged helmet. **8.** Turkish helmet as used on the Palestine Front. **9.** German 1916/17 sniper's face shield (weight 14½ pounds). **10.** Italian 1917 helmet, used mostly by shock troops and made of chrome-nickel steel. **11.** Franco-American 1917 Dunand helmet with visor

Uniforms of the First World War

Many of the armies which went to war in 1914 retained the colourful, flamboyant uniforms typical of the 19th century. These were soon adapted to the demands of modern war, however, and by 1918 uniforms had become drab and functional. In the following pages we illustrate a selection of the uniforms of the major combatants, along with a selection of the propaganda and recruiting posters which reflect the fascination exerted by the heraldry and regalia of war

National Bibliothek, Vienna

A picture of the time depicts Austro-Hungarian cavalry. Picturesque and superbly horsed, Austrian cavalry were an extravagant echo of the past

The nuts and bolts of mobilisation – the infantry division

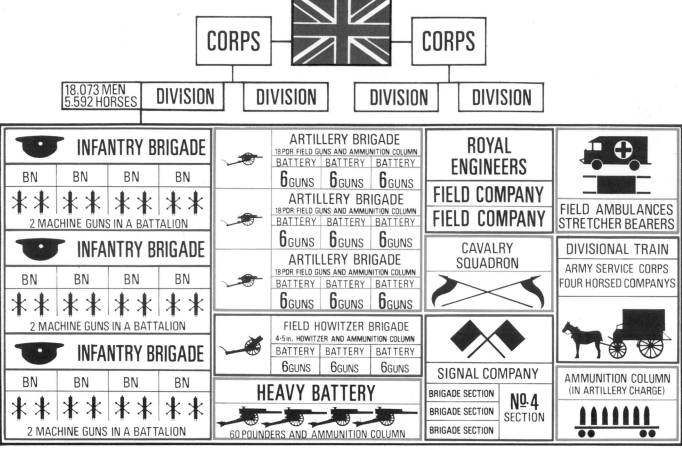

The smallest general command in 1914 was a division, and the infantry division was the standard component part of corps and armies. Here a British infantry division is compared with its German counterpart, both in strength and organisation

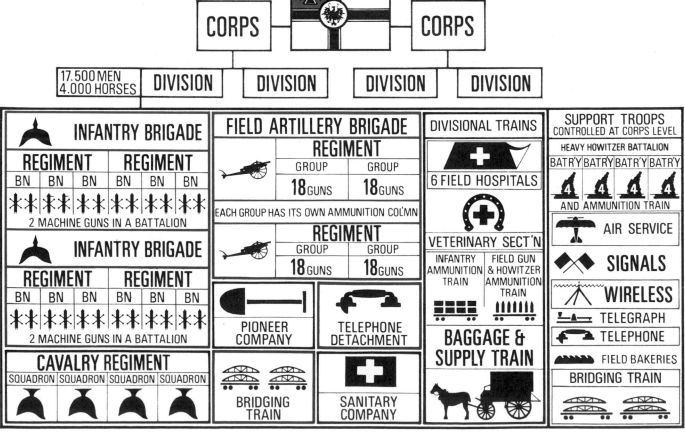

The German division, although numerically marginally smaller than the British, was much stronger in artillery, and had far more detailed and thorough logistical backing. It also had a larger cavalry detachment, and an air service

Concealment or display — the differing functions of uniforms in 1914

The British *khaki* uniform (left hand column) and the German *feld grau* (right hand column) compared favourably at merging into smoky, bracken and wooded backgrounds, and were, in fact, adequate in blending soldiers into the muddy and smoky battlegrounds. The French uniform, on the other hand, was not so satisfactory. The *horizon bleu* uniform (left centre column), issued during the winter of 1914, was certainly an improvement on the former red and dark blue (right centre column), but even so it was still not as good as the British and German uniforms

Jack Pia

German troops, agents of an aggressive nation's ambitions

A German hussar. Unlike his British counterpart he often carried a lance. As in other armies the German cavalry regarded themselves as an élite, but there was to be little scope for them in the coming war

A German artilleryman. Though less well equipped in light guns than his French opposite number, he was well provided with heavier field pieces

A German infantry-
man. Well trained and
enthusiastic, the
infantry formed the
backbone of the
German army

A Jäger, or rifleman.
More lightly equipped
than the standard
infantry of the line,
the Jäger regiments
were used for skirm-
ishing and scouting

Julian Allen

Left: A soldier of the German *Landsturm*. These third line troops were in the process of being re-equipped, so it is virtually impossible to describe a standard uniform. Nearly all photographic evidence indicates that they wore a mixture of old and new equipment. The shako is similar to the *Jäger* one, but taller and with the *Landsturm* badge on its front. *Right:* A German mountain soldier. These troops, often specially recruited from units in Bavaria or Württemberg, played an important part in the Serbian campaign. Their uniforms were simple and functional and unique in the German service. The cap was a standard *bergmütze* with hooked up side curtains and two fastening buttons in the front, the tunic and trousers were always grey, worn with heavy boots. *Opposite:* A poster depicting the Kaiser and the personification of the German *volk* united in helping their soldiers achieve 'just' political ends by military means.

Julian Allen

This poster reflects the changed attitudes towards the war. The accent is now on the defensive, on 'lasting out', in contrast to the stress placed on the offensive at the beginning of the war. The helmet too, and the equipment, reflect the demands of positional warfare, and appear modern in contrast to the uniforms and equipment of 1914

Storm troops — fast moving and hard hitting

Above: Firing hand grenades in a sap.
Right: A German storm trooper of 1918, carrying a Bergmann 9-mm 181 sub machine gun with snail-type magazine and stick bombs in two large canvas grenade bags. Wearing 1915 pattern steel helmet and grey-green jacket of *3rd Jäger Battalion* (the storm unit of *Second Army*), leather reinforced breeches, puttees and ankle boots. Entrenching tool and gas mask are carried behind. Small detachments of storm troops were maintained at battalion, regimental or divisional level, but the main body of storm troops was contained in 18 officially designated battalions, one being attached to each army

The French Armies

Ready, even over-eager, to fight,
French cavalry failed to form the essential links
between the armies, or even to act as effective
screens in front of them

Left: A French dragoon, equipped with a Lebel carbine and a wooden lance. His brass helmet was covered with felt to prevent it reflecting the sun and giving away his position. It had a horse-hair plume at the back. A groundsheet and blanket were also carried.

Right: A typical French infantryman equipped with a Lebel rifle. His bayonet handle is visible above his haversack and his coat, buttoned back to facilitate movement, hides the rest of the bayonet. The French infantry carried two leather ammunition pouches at the front, and a leather pack with a rigid frame at the back. A blanket, waterproof cape, a spare pair of boots and a mess tin were also carried in the pack. The pack was fastened at the top and the ends neatly rolled up.

Far right: A Belgian infantry NCO in battle order, with full pack and a Belgian Mauser Model 1889 7.65-mm rifle made by the FN factory.

Julian Allen

Left: A 'Blue Devil'—one of France's famous *Chasseurs Alpins,* skilled mountain troops. *Above:* France's mainstay in the desert: a private of the celebrated Foreign Legion.

Julian Allen

Julian Allen

French Lapel Badges:
the cult of Jingoism
reaches its limits

During the First World War, France
developed a booming industry in lapel
badges glorifying her successes — a sad
contrast with her bankruptcy in spirit
and in vigour during 1917. Among the
badges above are ones for the 75-mm
gun, the Chasseurs Alpins, Marshal Foch
and France's black colonial troops

FRANCE! BELGIQUE!

LIÈGE - Le Pont des Arches.
Le 7 Août 1914 - La Ville de LIÈGE par une défense
héroïque, repousse avec 35 000 HOMMES l'invasion de 120 000
ALLEMANDS". — La République Française lui confère la
Croix de la Légion d'honneur.

Above: A French poster awards the Belgian fortress of Liège the *Legion d'honneur* for its resistance to the Germans. But the red trousers and blue tunic so popular in French propaganda at the start of the war (see opposite) were highly impractical, and, by spring 1915, had been replaced by the *horizon bleu* uniform, *left,* issued in late 1914. *Right:* A French infantry private of 1917 in battle order—a *fusilier mitrailleur*, with a Chauchat 8-mm light machine gun.

Bapty

Julian Allen

Malcolm McGregor

Handkerchiefs with *motifs* of this kind were distributed freely to front-line troops. This one, in addition to giving the words and music of the *Marseillaise*, shows the flags and heads of state of the Entente nations. In the early stages of the war patriotic exhortations of this kind echoed the feelings of most of the serving troops, but as the war progressed and trench warfare conditions set in, this sort of 'flag-wagging' became increasingly out of touch with the feelings and motivation of the front line soldiers. In particular the picture of the scarlet-trousered soldiers charging with such *élan,* must have given rise to much sardonic comment

Above: One of the many reiterations of Austro-German brotherhood: the Kaiser and the Emperor Franz Josef, inappropriately framed in laurel leaves, smile out on the alliance of the two eagles. *Right:* In the shape of a cross France's plea to her people to reject Germany's claims on her land and bring in the dawn of her liberty. The German people are represented as a smilingly obsequious commercial traveller smugly pocketing France's liberties, in accordance with the grand German design of world domination. *Below:* A reminder of Allied loyalties but hardly of their achievements as the sun set on 1915. *Below right:* The colours of the Entente: Japan is now included in the line-up on a French cotton scarf.

France's colonial troops

The French Spahi. The Spahis were recruited from the native population of the French North African colony of Algeria, and were mostly born horsemen. As they were light cavalry, the Spahis carried little in the way of equipment, but what they did have was the standard French cavalry issue, worn with their colourful native dress. Apart from their sabres, they were armed with carbines, either the 8-mm 1886 Lebel, or the 1890/92 Berthier

The French Zouave. The Zouaves were recruited mostly from the white population of the French colonies of North Africa, and wore the traditional uniform shown here in the opening stages of the war. Their equipment and small arms were identical with those of ordinary infantry regiments of the line, and comprised a metal-framed pack (containing spare boots, great coat, blankets and mess tin), and the standard 8-mm 1886 Lebel rifle

For King and Country

British recruiting and propaganda posters tended to stress the fact that recruits were serving their king: in spite of this patriotic appeal, and the initial enthusiasm to join the ranks, the voluntary system was breaking down by 1916. 1 A poster stressing the importance of the factory worker's role in the war. 2 Many people saw the National Registration Act as the first step to compulsory service. 3 A naval recruiting poster. 4 A Scottish recruiting poster. The 'wee "scrap o' paper"' was the treaty guaranteeing Belgian neutrality which brought Britain into the war, dismissed as such by the Germans.

We're both needed to serve the Guns!

FILL UP THE RANKS! PILE UP THE MUNITIONS!

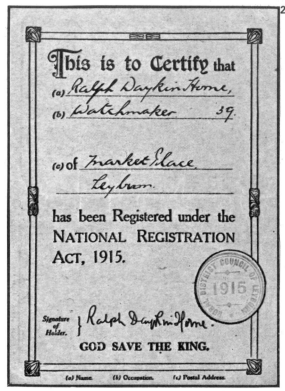

This is to Certify that
(a) Ralph Daykin Horne,
(b) Watchmaker 39.

(c) of Market Place
Leyburn.

has been Registered under the NATIONAL REGISTRATION ACT, 1915.

1915

Signature of Holder: Ralph Daykin Horne.

GOD SAVE THE KING.

(a) Name. (b) Occupation. (c) Postal Address.

G. R.
ROYAL NAVY
WANTED
SEAMEN
FOR THE PERIOD OF HOSTILITIES
(Continuous Service Rate of Pay)
Age - - 19 to 30
NO PREVIOUS EXPERIENCE NECESSARY—
but men with previous sea experience will be accepted up to the age of 38
Height - 5 ft. 4 ins.
Chest - - 35 ins.
Separation Allowance at Naval Rates

YOUR KING & COUNTRY NEED YOU

A WEE "SCRAP O' PAPER" IS BRITAIN'S BOND.

TO MAINTAIN THE HONOUR AND GLORY OF THE BRITISH EMPIRE

The BEF — a drop in the ocean in terms of fighting strength to the French, but concrete proof of Britain's resolve to support her ally

Above: A British cavalryman was equipped with a Lee Enfield rifle, shown here in a leather gun bucket. But his primary weapon was still the long bamboo lance with a metal tip, which was both strong and flexible. He also had a groundsheet, a horse blanket under the saddle and a water bottle on his back.
Above right: A British infantryman, shown here on the march and not as he would appear on parade. The scale of infantry equipment in the BEF included the Lee Enfield SMLE No 1 Mk. 3 rifle, personal ammunition and an entrenching tool. The infantry had almost completed the change from leather to webbing and the belt, ammunition pouches, and water bottle carrier were all made of webbing.

Julian Allen

Kriegs Weihnacht 1914

Above: A German Christmas poster of 1914. *Below:* A nostalgic reminder of home on the Eastern Front as nurses join Russians and Germans in a Christmas truce. *Right:* A German infantryman in the winter of 1914/15. The uniform was unchanged from August except that helmet numerals, if retained, were in green rather than red. Officers wore light grey greatcoats and other ranks dark grey. These two shades should not be confused with *feld grau*. Other comforts, such as knitted gloves and balaclava helmets, had to be supplied by relatives at home

Imperial War Museum

Above: Princess Mary's Christmas gift to British troops. *Below:* Highland troops strengthen their barbed wire defences during the Christmas truce. The Germans are only 40 yards away. *Left:* A Highlander in winter equipment. Arms and equipment were ordinary infantry issue, but in the winter of 1914, Highland units changed from shoes with half gaiters and stockings to boots and half puttees as these were more suitable in the trenches. Most units were also issued with Field Service caps, but the troops preferred balaclava helmets

Each soldier carried 66 lbs of equipment, making it difficult to get out of a trench, impossible to move faster than a slow walk, impossible to rise or lie down quickly

Every infantryman on the first day of the Somme wore 'fighting order' consisting of the normal equipment including steel helmet and entrenching tool, less the pack and greatcoat; with rolled ground sheet, water-bottle and haversack in place of the pack on the back. In the haversack were small things, mess tin, towel, shaving kit, extra socks, message book, 'the unconsumed portion of the days ration'. Two gas helmets and tear goggles were carried, also wire cutters, field dressing, iodine, 220 rounds of ammunition, two sand bags and two Mills grenades. The total weight carried per man was about 66 lbs. **1** towel. **2** 'housewife'. **3** extra socks. **4** soap. **5** iron rations. **6** preserved rations. **7** canvas holdall containing comb, shaving kit, etc.

Julian Allen

BRITAIN · NEEDS

YOU · AT · ONCE

Right: A soldier of the Imperial Camel Corps Brigade, which included British, Australian, New Zealand and Indian troops. There was a considerable degree of individualism in the dress and equipment of members of the Brigade, who often used Arab items as well as British

Julian Allen

Malcolm McGregor

A Bedouin tribesman. His head is covered with a *keffiyeh*, bound with an *agal*, a double coil of goat hair

Below: Soldiers of the Indian Army. *From left to right:* A sepoy of the 2nd Gurkha Rifles, a sepoy of the 4th Gurkha Rifles, wearing service kit, a sowar (Sikh) of the 11th Bengal Lancers, a sepoy of the 15th Ludhiana Sikhs, a sepoy of the 26th Punjabis (Pathan).

Background: An Indian column in France 1914. *Foreground:* A British Captain of Indian Infantry. Leg and foot wear was identical to British issue, but the head-dress and tunic differed. The head-dress was a khaki Wolsey-pattern cork helmet

Barry Evans

In Hindustani and Urdu, this British recruiting poster made a
very simple yet effective appeal to Indians: food for their
families, good pay, free clothing and the minimum of danger.
Naturally it does not deal with that other reality for the
Indian who soldiered in 1915: the horrific chaos in Mesopotamia

Above: A British infantryman in typical hot weather Mesopotamia gear. *Left:* A Sikh infantryman, Suez 1915. The Sikh regiments wore the standard 'shirt-tunics', trousers and puttees, but with a leather bandolier around the waist. *Right:* A Gurkha soldier with his .303 SMLE rifle. The bayonet was worn on the left hip, the kukri on the right.

Julian Allen

45

Opponents in Africa

Right: An NCO of the *Kaiserlich Schutztruppe* (German colonial troops) wearing the standard service dress with traditional cork sun helmet. *Opposite, left:* A Commando, 1914 style. The South African forces in 1914 were raised from both the British and Afrikaans sections of the population. The Afrikaans units were organised in Commandos, and in many cases each man was expected to supply his own weapon and horse. A variety of rifles were used, including German Mausers. *Right:* An Askari. The uniform and equipment worn by these soldiers were usually modified to suit the particular conditions of war; the puttees and boots, for example, were frequently discarded. This Askari carries his rolled blanket on his back; his rifle would be an SMLE .303.

Julian Allen

A New Zealand soldier wearing a British pattern uniform with a simple brass NZ shoulder badge. It was after Gallipoli that the New Zealanders' bush hat was worn shaped to a point — to distinguish them from their Australian counterparts

An Australian soldier wearing the standard field service dress, comprising a loose-fitting tunic and a bush hat. The Australians disliked conventional uniforms and always adapted them to suit fighting and climatic conditions

THE EMPIRE NEEDS MEN!

AUSTRALIA
CANADA
INDIA
NEW ZEALAND

All answer the call.

Helped by the YOUNG LIONS
The OLD LION defies his Foes.

ENLIST NOW.

'GOD BLESS DADDY'
45,000 AUSTRALIAN FATHERS ARE FIGHTING!
WILL YOU HELP?

1 Maori butcher at his work in France.
2 Australian recruiting poster. In the earlier part of the war as many as 12,000 Australians volunteered each month.
3 Canadians at the time of the battle of the Somme tend German wounded

Boys Come over here you're wanted

4 Australian poster asking for recruits for Gallipoli. 5 West Indians clean their rifles on the road to Amiens. 6 Appeal for money for a European war from the hungry people of British India. Poster says 'Give money to help our warriors'

युद्ध ऋणमें कर्ज दो,

जिससे लड़ाई जितने में सहायता हो।

Italy goes to War

When the war broke out many Italians wanted to join their allies, Germany and Austria-Hungary. One enthusiastic general suggested mobilizing troops and sending them to the Rhine. But as the months went by, public opinion in Italy changed, and after a year of diplomatic manoeuvrings, torchlight demonstrations, doubt, and bewilderment, Italy declared war—and forces were sent to fight Austria instead

Below: 'The Intervention', an ironic painting by Aldo Carpi. The red flag of socialism and the white flag of reaction greet Italy's entry into the war against her former allies. Overleaf: Italian propaganda map showing in red the Italian-speaking areas still occupied by Austria. In the top left corner the figures representing Trento and Trieste, 'the unredeemed lands', wait mourning for Italia (centre) to redeem them from their chains. Over the heads of the soldiers hover the great figures of the Risorgimento, Garibaldi, Victor Emmanuel, Mazzini, and Cavour.

CARTA SIMBOLICO-GE[OGRAFICA]

Trieste e Trento
simbolo di dolore

G. OBERDAN
fatto impiccare da Francesco Giuseppe
a Trieste per sentire italianamente
il 1882 a soli 24 anni.

Italia! Italia! non fu mai tuo maggio
nella città del Fiore e del Leone
quando ogni fiato era d'amor messaggio,

sì novo come questa tua stagione
maravigliosa in cui per te si canta
con la bocca rotonda del cannone.

Emerge dalle sacre acque di Lissa

RE D'ITALIA

	Battalions	Batteries	Cavalry Squadrons	Dreadnoughts	Pre Dreadnoughts	Destroyers and Cruisers	Aircraft
Italy	549	434	166	6	15	62	79
Austria-Hungary	234	155	21	4	12	35	136

Julian Allen.

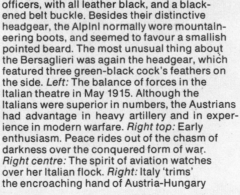

Raccolta Bertarelli/Milan

Musée des Trois Guerres

Above: Five Italian soldiers. From left to right, an infantry officer, an artilleryman, an Alpino, an infantryman and a Bersagliere. These uniforms are basically the 1908 Service Dress, which became standard at the beginning of the war, although some units did continue to wear an obsolete pattern. The colour of the uniforms illustrated approximated closely to that of the German *Jäger.* The markings for distinguishing between the various arms of the army were the differing colours of the patches on each soldier's collar and, of course, the headgear of the Alpini and Bersaglieri. At first, equipment was blackened leather (later natural brown), buff canvas and brown boots. The officer depicted, a captain of the 11th Regiment, Casale Brigade, is typical of Italian

officers, with all leather black, and a blackened belt buckle. Besides their distinctive headgear, the Alpini normally wore mountaineering boots, and seemed to favour a smallish pointed beard. The most unusual thing about the Bersaglieri was again the headgear, which featured three green-black cock's feathers on the side. *Left:* The balance of forces in the Italian theatre in May 1915. Although the Italians were superior in numbers, the Austrians had advantage in heavy artillery and in experience in modern warfare. *Right top:* Early enthusiasm. Peace rides out of the chasm of darkness over the conquered form of war. *Right centre:* The spirit of aviation watches over her Italian flock. *Right:* Italy 'trims' the encroaching hand of Austria-Hungary

The range of uniforms worn by the Austro-Hungarian army during the First World War. *This page, left to right. First left:* A *Wachtmeister* (Warrant Officer) from the Honved Hussar Regiment, 1914 to 1915. *Second left:* A *Stabswachtmeister* (Warrant Officer 1st Class) from the 3rd Ulane Regiment, 1914 to 1915. *Third left:* Trooper of the 15th Dragoon Regiment, 1914 to 1915. *Fourth left:* A *Gefreiter* (Lance-Corporal) of the 4th Infantry Regiment, 1914 to 1915.

This page, left to right. First left: An officer of less than staff rank in an artillery regiment, 1915 to 1918. *Second left:* A rifleman from a rifle regiment, carrying alpine equipment and dressed for mountainous conditions, 1917 to 1918. *Third*

left: A rifleman from an infantry regiment, 1916 to 1918, with an Austrian steel helmet and full winter equipment. *Fourth left:* A Stormtrooper of 1918, kitted out with German steel helmet, light equipment, respirator and grenades

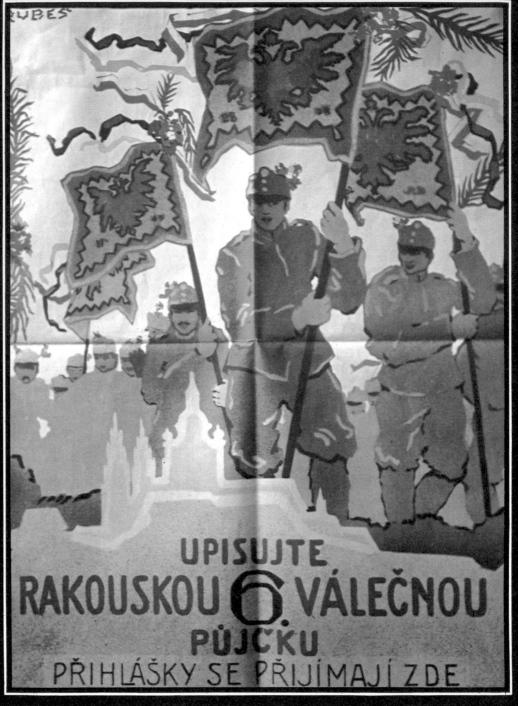

An Austro-Hungarian war loan poster, printed in Czech. Such appeals, though successful in raising money for the war effort, also served to highlight the ethnic difficulties of the army, and thus aided the nationalistic ambitions of strong separatist groups such as the Czechs: 'They appeal to us for money, but our men are led into battle by officers who speak only German or Hungarian'

Adversaries in the Balkans

When Austria attacked Serbia in August 1914, her military leaders expected a walk-over. The Serbs, however, although outnumbered and lacking in arms and equipment, had much valuable experience of battle, and a skilful high command. *Left:* An infantryman of the Austro-Hungarian forces. His formal military training did not compensate for the Serbian soldier's more recent experience of battle. *Right:* A Serbian infantryman. In fact, a Serbian soldier would have been fortunate to find himself as fully equipped as this. Some of those called upon to defend their country could not even be supplied with rifles. They might, however, be veterans of the two Balkan wars and many other less official clashes with the Turks. *Below:* An Austrian cavalryman in the field-grey tunic and iron-grey breeches which were introduced in 1915 and were standard uniform by 1916. His belt and equipment were still of leather.

Left: A Bulgarian officer. The tunic was grey-brown, the trousers grey. *Right:* A Bulgarian infantryman. There were considerable variations both in the way that the uniform was worn and in the parts of a uniform issued to each man. This illustration shows the brown fatigue uniform, the standard Bulgarian field service uniform of the First World War. Boots were worn, but characteristic of the Bulgars were the *opankers*, national peasant footwear. Equipment was usually of the German pre-1908 pattern (leather). *Below:* A Czechoslovak legionary, wearing mainly Russian uniform, but with the cap distinctive to the legion. The rifle is a Japanese Asaka, as supplied in large quantities to Russia in 1914.

Julian Allan

HOR SA DO ŠÍKU! BRAT K BRATOVI STAŇME,

SEM K NAM! SLOVAKA MENO KTO NOSI!

VOJÁK ČESKOSLOVENSKÉ ARMÁDY VE FRANCII

HOJ OTČINA! OTČINA!

ZBIŤ LEBO MRIEŤ!

VOJÁK ČESKOSLOVENSKÉ
: ARMÁDY VE FRANCII :

BRATŘE V AMERICE! PROČ SE

NEHLÁSÍŠ K NAŠÍ ARMÁDĚ..?

VOJÁK ČESKOSLOVENSKÉ
ARMÁDY VE FRANCII

Brothers in America!
Fight for
Czechoslovakia
on the French front

By 1918 there were Czechoslovak units fighting
on the French, Russian and Italian fronts,
and in each of these countries recruiting
organisations issued postcards appealing for
volunteers. Shown here are American and
Russian examples. The Russian cards (opposite
and bottom centre) not unnaturally appeal in
Russian for recruits for the Russian front,
while the American cards (all the remainder)
use the Czech language to inspire Czech-
American patriots to fight in France. When
the war began, Masaryk believed that only
liberation by the Russian armies could create
favourable conditions for the establishment
of a Czechoslovak state, but the reverses
suffered by the Russians in the field soon
destroyed this illusion. Increasingly he
pinned his hopes on the Western Allies, but
at first they would not listen to him: they
had gone to war not to destroy the Habsburg
monarchy but to maintain the balance of power,
of which Austria-Hungary was an integral part.
By the end of 1916, however, they had swung
behind the cause of Czechoslovak independence

JIŽ VZHŮRU ČESKÝ SOKOLE!

VLAST VOLÁ! MĚJ SE K ČINU!

VOJÁK ČESKOSLOVENSKÉ
: ARMÁDY VE FRANCII

ČESKOSLOVEN. ARMÁDA v RUSKU

V SRDCI ZPĚV, V RUCE ZBRAŇ,
VLAST SVOU PROTI VRAHŮM CHRAŇ!

KU PŘEDU! KU PŘEDU!

ZPÁTKY NI KROK!

VOJÁK ČESKOSLOVENSKÉ
: ARMÁDY VE FRANCII :

Above: Serbian cavalry. *Left* and *right:* Private in the Serbian army. After the retreat and virtual annihilation of the Serbian army in 1915 the survivors had fled to Corfu. There they were gradually reassembled and provided with French equipment, their uniforms a combination of French and traditional Serbian cut. Rifles issued to the Serbs were the Mauser, 8-mm Lebel, and 8-mm Mannlicher-Berthier.

Left: An Austrian artilleryman. There was little standardisation in the uniforms worn by these soldiers: puttees often replaced the thick, oiled woollen socks, the gold stars on the collar were often obscured by a grey handkerchief tied around the neck.
Right: A Montenegrin infantryman wearing the uniform which was standardised only just before the war. In fact, most Montenegrin soldiers wore a traditional, rather flamboyànt costume.

Julian Allen

Left: A Turkish infantryman. The design of Turkish uniforms was strongly influenced by German advisers. This soldier wears the traditional *Kabalash* hat, a Khaki tunic with flap-down collar, khaki trousers and puttees wound from the boots up. His equipment is also of German pattern. *Above:* A Turkish cavalryman. The uniform of the Turkish cavalry was similar to that worn by the infantry. The main differences were the single large box pouch worn on either side of the belt instead of the three small box pouches, and the knee-high boots, which were usually black. *Opposite:* The uniforms of a Greek officer and infantryman. The infantryman is shown wearing the field service uniform of 1912, but often there was much non-conformity as regards dress. By a curious assortment of regulation and private clothing the volunteers managed to appear more like the Montenegrins than the Greek regular forces, and when the French made available a large quantity of equipment and helmets, the situation was further confused. They were armed with the 6.5-mm Mannlicher Schoenauer M 1903/14 rifle, and were also supplied with a number of French weapons including the 8-mm Lebel and Mannlicher-Berthier rifles.

Malcolm McGregor

Poles at War

Before the establishment of a Polish State, which after a prolonged struggle was finally recognised officially in 1923, Poles served largely in other men's armies. Illustrated are Poles serving in the Austrian lancers (left), the Russian cavalry (right), and the French army (below).

Malcolm McGregor

The badge of a unit in the Polish Legion. The
Legion had its origins before the war, when Josef
Piłsudski, the Polish nationalist leader, realised
that if war between the Great Powers was to occur
Polish aspirations might be helped by the presence
in the field of an independent Polish military
force. As early as 1908 he founded the 'League of
Active Struggle' which organised and trained military
units. By the outbreak of war Piłsudski could
put nearly 7,000 armed men in the field, mainly
recruited from Austrian Poland

The Japanese soldier

Right: A Japanese infantryman in his basic standard issue uniform carrying an Arisaka Model 38/1905 6.5-mm rifle. The colour of the uniform had been changed from blue to green as a result of the lessons learned from the Russo-Japanese War of 1904/05. The only way in which it was possible to distinguish between the various branches of the army was by the colour of the collar patch—red was the colour of the infantry. *Left:* A Japanese infantryman in his standard winter service dress. The Japanese were unique among the combatant powers of the First World War in issuing their troops with both greatcoats and mackintoshes in the winter. The latter was worn over the former, and thus the wearer was kept both warm and dry—in theory.

Julian Allen

Russian soldiers: formidable individually, but collectively ill-organised and poorly equipped

◁ A Russian infantry-man armed with the M 1891 Moisin-Nagent 7.62-mm rifle. Although scabbards were issued it was common practice to have the bayonet permanently fixed. The *kittel* or smock shown in both illustrations was a campaign uniform worn by all branches of the Russian army

▷ A Russian cavalry-man. The cavalry were issued with either the M 1891 dragoon rifle or the M 1910 Moisin-Nagent, both 7.62-mm. Again the *kittel* is shown, but otherwise there was little standardisation of uniforms and equip-ment in the Russian army during this period of re-organisation

Barry Evans

Russia's multiracial Empire — now in the grip of the most profound political revolution of the century

The Russian Empire, occupying the larger part of the Asian land mass, was as diverse racially as any in the world. For the average Mongolian or Kirghiz, Petrograd was as remote as London was for a native African. Nor was European Russia any less diverse; Armenians, Ukrainians, the people of the Baltic seaboard — all owed allegiance to the Tsar. All these people had borne their share in the war alongside 'pure' Russians, and now the revolution was to change for ever the social order under which they had lived. We show here a selection of the peoples of the Russian Empire, taken from a book published after the First World War in Germany, entitled *Germany's Enemies in the World War*. **1.** A Great Russian from the northern and Baltic regions of Russia. **2.** Two Armenians from Trans-Caucasia. **3.** Muscovite. **4.** Ruthenian. **5.** A Jew from the Caucasus. **6.** Tartar. **7.** Siberians from Amur (first or second generation settlers in Siberia of Russian extraction). **8.** Three Georgians. **9.** A more common German view of what Siberians were like. **10.** A Ukrainian. **11.** A Tartar from the Perm area in the Urals. **12.** A Don Cossack. **13.** Tartars from Mongolia. **14.** A Chuvash from Finnish Russia *(left)*, a Cherremis, also from Finnish Russia *(right)*, and a Bashkir from the Urals *(centre)*

Above: The Cossacks formed the greater part of Russia's effective cavalry forces. Born horsemen, they were formidable adversaries. They were renowned rifle shots, but really came into their own when they charged with their sabres. Tough, hardy men, they were capable of living off the country. The uniform was based on the traditional Cossack clothing. *Left:* A Russian artilleryman, wearing the distinctive dark-green trousers. *Right:* A Russian cavalry officer in standard uniform.

I WANT YOU
FOR U.S. ARMY
NEAREST RECRUITING STATION

Left: A fighting sergeant in the American infantry, wearing the fighting dress adopted in late 1917. He has a British steel helmet and British-style gas mask case and puttees. The revolver carried would have been either a Colt 45 or a Smith and Wesson 38. *Opposite:* A US artillery captain. *Background:* 'To the Victor belong the Spoils'. American soldiers with a prisoner collecting German equipment as trophies, in September 1918, drawn by George Harding.

'America, the daughter of Europe, crossed the ocean to wrest her mother . . . . . . from the humiliation of thralldom and to save civilisation.'

Julian Allan

Culver Pictures Inc.

Culver Pictures Inc.

76

Antagonists in Mexico — the disciplined and better equipped troops of the United States against the irregular cavalry of Mexico, divided as much against each other as against the invading Americans

Far left: An American cavalry trooper. *Left above:* A Mexican border raider. By their very nature the raiders were independent of any central authority, and were as much trouble to the various Mexican governments as to the United States. *Left below:* Pascual Orozco, Madero's former chief general and a bitter enemy of Villa. *Below:* The celebrated Pancho Villa (holding the Hotchkiss machine gun) with one of his followers. *Right:* Another famous figure—Emiliano Zapata, from Mexico's southern province

Culver Pictures Inc.

Brown Brothers

The Unknown Warrior

Two years after the war had ended a strange, emotional, even macabre ceremony was
performed in the streets of London. It served as a focal point for all the feelings of guilt and
loss that still lingered from the war, and although it was imitated by several other
nations, no other ceremony had quite the poignancy of the burial of the Unknown
Warrior in Westminster on Armistice Day, 1920.

The idea originated in the mind of a young army chaplain, the Rev David Railton, who
wrote to the Dean of Westminster Abbey suggesting that the body of an unidentified
British soldier should be buried in the Abbey as a symbol of the nation's loss. After some
caution the idea was taken up and, in France, a blindfold officer chose one of six
unidentified bodies from the battlefields. From France the body travelled to Dover and
then to London. As its journey progressed, national interest and excitement grew. At
Dover it received a 19-gun salute. From Dover it travelled in a special carriage to London,
and rested overnight at Victoria Station. On the next morning, November 11, the coffin
was collected by the pallbearers: five Admirals, four Field Marshals and two Generals.
Among them were Haig, Beatty and Wilson. One of the war's most obscure victims was
borne slowly through the London streets by the war's greatest leaders and organisers,
followed on foot by the King Emperor of the largest Empire in the world's history, bearing
a wreath with a card inscribed in his own appalling writing. The procession was watched
by packed, silent crowds. The state funeral of an unknown man provided the occasion for
thousands of separate individual griefs

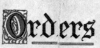

Army Orders

BY
GENERAL SIR H. S. RAWLINSON, BART.
K.C.B., K.C.V.O., COMMANDING FOURTH ARMY

IMMEDIATE REWARDS.

Under authority delegated by His Majesty the King, the Field Marshal Commanding-in-Chief has made the following awards for gallantry and devotion to duty in action :—

THE MILITARY MEDAL.

No. 12821 A/Sergeant A. E. IDE, Royal Field Artillery.
No. 39492 Sergeant T. J. SOUTHEY, Royal Field Artillery.
No. 2518 L/Corporal A. CHELL, Notts. and Derby Regiment.
No. 3154 A/Corporal D. McLAREN, Argyll and Sutherland Highlanders.

MERITORIOUS SERVICE MEDAL.

Under authority delegated by his Majesty the King, the Field Marshal Commanding-in-Chief has awarded the Meritorious Service Medal (without additional pension) to—

No. 17893 Private R. CALDWELL, Loyal North Lancashire Regiment.

for conspicuous bravery, presence of mind and promptitude in averting a grenade accident whilst at drill.

Under authority delegated by the Field Marshal Commanding-in-Chief, Corps Commanders have made the following awards for gallantry and devotion to duty in action :—

BAR TO THE MILITARY MEDAL.

No. 16788 Sergeant T. LEWINS, Somerset Light Infantry.
No. 68875 Private (A/Corporal) H. STORRY, Royal Army Medical Corps.

THE MILITARY MEDAL.

No. 66144 Gunner H. CLOAD, Royal Garrison Artillery.
No. 318560 Gunner E. J. LEACH, Royal Garrison Artillery.
No. 83211 Sergeant T. G. BULLIVANT, Royal Garrison Artillery.
No. 48840 L/Corporal E. REED, Royal Engineers.
No. 49772 Corporal J. HAMILTON, Royal Engineers.
No. 48835 Sergeant W. BEE, Royal Engineers.
No. 31308 Private R. EDWARDS, King's (Liverpool Regiment).
No. 14021 L/Corporal (A/Cpl.) E. DENNETT, Lincolnshire Regiment.
No. 16870 Private E SAUNDERS, Somerset Light Infantry.
No. 7274 Private B STOCK, Lancashire Fusiliers.
No. 281252 Private J. DAVIES, Lancashire Fusiliers.
No. 240080 Sergeant A COOPEY, Gloucestershire Regiment (T.F.)
No. 241000 Corporal R. BUTT, Gloucestershire Regiment (T.F.)
No. 265296 Private H. CROSS, Oxford and Bucks Light Infantry.
No. 265405 Sergeant S. T. H. WOODHAM, Oxford and Bucks Light Infantry.
No. 200774 Private (L/Cpl.) G. J. LEEDS, Oxford and Bucks Light Infantry.
No. 201129 Private R. G. CHAMINGS, Oxford and Bucks Light Infantry.
No. 203382 Private A. W. MAY, Oxford and Bucks Light Infantry.
No. 200631 Sergeant H. A. HARRIS, Oxford and Bucks Light Infantry.
No. 200602 Corporal G. AMBEREY, Oxford and Bucks Light Infantry.
No. 201116 Private (L/Cpl.) R. J. COLLIER, Oxford and Bucks Light Infantry.
No. 201472 Private E. AYRES, Oxford and Bucks Light Infantry.
No. 205461 Private A. HERBERT, Oxford and Bucks Light Infantry.
No. 267585 Private F. G. SEWARD, Oxford and Bucks Light Infantry.
No. 305892 L/Sergeant E. BILTON, Sherwood Foresters.
No. 37498 Private W. P. SMITH, Royal Berkshire Regiment.
No. 11722 Sergeant H. STAMP, Royal Berkshire Regiment.
No. 17355 Private G. GRAHAM, Royal Berkshire Regiment.
No. G/15385 Private G. CLARK, Middlesex Regiment.
No. G/1810 Private J. H. BEER, Middlesex Regiment.
No. G/19967 Private T. JOBSON, Middlesex Regiment.
No. R/7844 Sergeant R. WILLIAMS, King's Royal Rifle Corps.
No. R/682 L/Corporal P. H. ALDRIDGE, King's Royal Rifle Corps.
No. 735 L/Corporal R. FRIER, King's Royal Rifle Corps.
No. 811 Sergeant R. G. ELKINTON, King's Royal Rifle Corps.
No. 8519 Rifleman J. RAWLINSON, King's Royal Rifle Corps.
No. 1508 Rifleman H. DUGMORE, King's Royal Rifle Corps.
No. 10458 Rifleman C. KEYWORTH, King's Royal Rifle Corps.
No. S/25477 Rifleman S. SANDFORD, Rifle Brigade.
No. S/12702 Rifleman W. D. GRAVES, Rifle Brigade.
No. S/449 Rifleman T. FALLON, Rifle Brigade.
No. B/200346 Corporal G. SMITH, Rifle Brigade.
No. S/5630 Corporal H. FARMER, Rifle Brigade.
No. B/200441 Corporal F. GOODING, Rifle Brigade.
No. 68894 Private W. UTTLEY, Royal Army Medical Corps.

May 4th, 1917.

H. C. HOLMAN, *Major-General,*
D.A. & Q.M.G., Fourth Army.

Headquarters, Fourth Army,
4th June, 1917.

To No.318560 Gunner E. J. LEACH,
Royal Garrison Artillery.

I congratulate you on the gallant act by which you have won the

MILITARY MEDAL.

H. Rawlinson Genl.
Cmg. Fourth Army.

FOR VALOUR
AND JUST BEING THERE
MEDALS OF THE FIRST WORLD WAR

Medals are the tokens of a nation's esteem. They are awarded in time of war and in time of peace for acts of exceptional gallantry and valour, and for services to the war effort or to the well-being of the nation.

We are here concerned with the medals awarded in time of war. These fall into three categories: those for valour, those for 'just being there' and those for services rendered.

The first category comprises the world's most famous and coveted medals: the British Victoria Cross, the United States' Medal of Honour and the senior awards of other countries. In some nations, the medal for outstanding bravery and that for great services were one and the same. Take, for example, the highest award Germany could bestow, the *Pour le Mérite*. Although it was awarded to men who had performed great and valiant acts in the field, it was also given to generals and other men in recognition of their conduct of the war or of other signal services. In this respect, the Pour le Mérite can

be regarded as a cross between the Victoria Cross, awarded for acts of singular gallantry, and the Companion of the Bath, conferred for services to the war effort or particular success in the field of command or direction.

The second category, that for 'just being there', is made up of the campaign medals. Whereas gallantry decorations are usually in the form of a cross, the campaign medals are usually circular in form, and awarded to men who have taken part in a specific campaign. These are awarded without reference to a man's performance, but merely in recognition of the fact that a soldier or sailor has been involved in a particular campaign. This is not to belittle the rôle of the ordinary soldier, for without him the war could not have been fought, and against his deeds must be measured those of the 'heroes'.

The third category, that of services rendered, always resulted in wry amusement for the ordinary soldier. To him, 'base wallahs' were decorated for incompetence,

if not for outright theft of the line soldiers' rations and equipment. The attitude is understandable, but largely erroneous. Without these 'base wallahs', no army could have survived. They were labouring under unforeseen difficulties, and were therefore inadequately trained, and inexperienced, and often deserved the DSOs and other decorations they received.

It is worth noting that the Allies were far more prolific with the institution and award of medals. The Germans, in particular, had two national medals only. Others were struck by the states making up the Empire for their own contingents, and still others were struck for particular events, such as the 1914 advance on Paris, but on the whole, the Central wero restricted themselves to a few all-embracing medals.

Left: A French investiture. Note the regimental flags in the background. *Below:* The United States' Medal of Honour. Illustrated is the Army version — the Navy's is similar, but the medal is suspended from an anchor, not a bar

Top row, left to right:
Great Britain. Britain's highest award for gallantry, the Victoria Cross. This is a cross *pattée*, in bronze, suspended from a claret ribbon. 633 were awarded in the First World War, 187 of them posthumously; the Distinguished Service Order, awarded only to commissioned officers; the Military Cross, instituted on December 31, 1914, and awarded to warrant officers and above; the Distinguished Flying Cross, instituted in December 1918 and awarded retrospectively to officers and warrant officers of the RAF; the Air Force Cross, the same as the DFC, but awarded for acts of bravery not necessarily in the face of the enemy; the Distinguished Conduct Medal, awarded to NCOs and men only. The Distinguished Service Medal, instituted in October 1914 for petty officers and men of the RN and NCOs and men of the Royal Marines.
Centre row, left to right:
The Military Medal, instituted in March 1916, and the equivalent of the MC for NCOs and men; the Indian Distinguished Service Medal (reverse). Its award was extended in July 1917 to Indian non-combatants on field service; the Meritorious Service Medal (Army); the 1914 Star, with the '5th Aug-22nd Nov 1914' bar, awarded to those who were actually under fire during that period; the 1914-1915 Star; the British War Medal; the Victory Medal.
Bottom row, left to right:
The United States of America. The distinguished Service Cross (Army), second pattern. This cross was awarded to any member of the army, regardless of rank, who 'shall have distinguished himself or herself by extraordinary heroism'; the Navy Cross, the US Navy's and Marine Corps' equivalent of the DSC; the Distinguished Service Medal (Army), awarded for 'exceptionally meritorious service'; the Silver Star, awarded to indicate 'a citation for gallantry in action' . . .; the Distinguished Flying Cross, for aviators who had been recommended for, but had not been awarded, other high medals; Queen Mary decorates a sailor; the US Victory Medal

Imperial War Museum

Top row, left to right:
France. The Légion d'Honneur, France's highest decoration. This is awarded only for gallantry in action or 20 years' distinguished service in military or civilian life. Illustrated is the badge of an *Officier,* the fourth of the five grades; the Médaille Militaire, awarded only to generals commanding armies, admirals commanding fleets and NCOs in the army or navy; the Croix de Guerre, instituted in April 1915 and awarded to soldiers and sailors of all ranks mentioned in despatches by a general or CO; the Croix de Guerre des Théatres d'Opérations Extériers. The Médaille de la Reconnaissance Française, awarded from 1917 on for acts of devotion in the public interest. Illustrated is an example of the highest of the three classes, in silver gilt; the Médaille Commémorative de la Grande Guerre, for all mobilised during the war; the Médaille Interalliée dite 'De la Victoire'.

Centre row, left to right:
Médaille d'Orient; the Médaille des Dardanelles. The different ribbons of these medals were decided upon at the request of those who had served in the Dardanelles; the Médaille des Evadés, for escaped POWs; the Croix du Combattant, for all holders of a combatant's card; the Croix du Combattant Volontaire, for those who volunteered for service; the Ordre de la Mérite Maritime (obverse), 3rd Class.
Montenegro. The Order of Danilo, third of the five classes.

Bottom row, left to right:
Imperial Russia. The Cross of St George, 3rd Class, awarded only for gallantry in action; the Order of St Anne, 2nd Class. When awarded for military services, the cross had crossed swords between its limbs; the Order of St Stanislas, 2nd Class, without swords; the Order of St Vladimir, 3rd Class, with swords.
Japan. The Order of the Rising Sun, 4th of eight classes, awarded to all ranks of the army and navy for gallantry; the Order of the Second Treasure, 4th of eight classes, awarded for meritorious service; the Victory Medal.

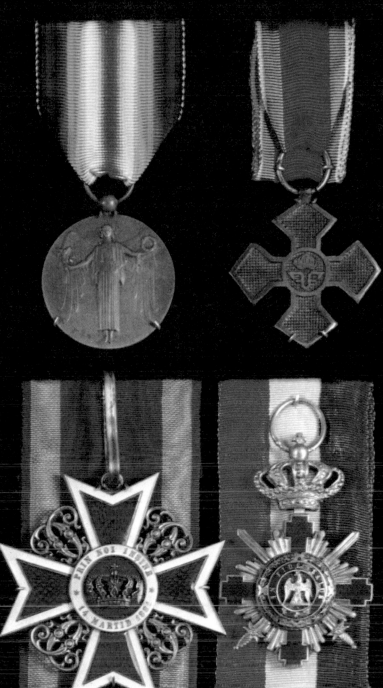

Kaiser Wilhelm II decorates one of his soldiers. There were only two German awards open to all, the Iron Cross and the Pour le Mérite. Each member state of the Empire struck its own medals

Top row, left to right:
Italy. The Order of St Maurice and St Lazarus, 5th Class; the Order of the Crown of Italy, 5th Class; the War Cross; the War Medal (two bars).
Czechoslovakia. The Revolutionary Cross.
Portugal. The Victory Medal.
Rumania. The War Cross.

Centre row, left to right:
Belgium. The Order of Leopold I, 5th of five classes, with swords. It was awarded to officers for gallantry and long service, and to NCOs for professional services; the Order of Leopold II, 4th Class; the Order of the Crown, 4th Class; the Croix de Guerre. It was awarded for the same deeds as its French counterpart, and also for long service.
Rumania. The Order of the Crown, 3rd Class; the Order of the Star, 5th Class with swords.

Bottom row, left to right:
Greece. The War Cross. This was at first solely Venizelist, but was later adopted nationally. It was granted only for gallantry initially, but later for war services in general. Illustrated is the 3rd of three classes: the Medal of Military Merit, 4th Class.
Serbia. The Order of St Sava, 5th Class; the Order of Takowa, 3rd Class.
Poland. The Order of Military Virtue, 5th of five classes; the Cross of Valour (with a Second World War ribbon).
Germany. The Pour le Mérite, Germany's highest award; the Iron Cross, 2nd Class.

ARMY, CORPS & DIVISIONAL FLASHES

The British, early in the war, felt the need to identify the transport and personnel of the formations of the army, the BEF in particular. Initially this took the form of armlets and boards with the number of the particular formation upon it. But this was poor for security, so badges were instituted, either painted on signs or sewn on uniforms. Basically there were five types of badge or sign in use in the First World War:

● Distinctive signs with no particular origin or meaning;
● Territorial signs such as the thistle of the 9th (Scottish) Division;
● Cypher signs;
● Puns on the GOC's name; and
● Battle honour signs, such as the umbrella of the 54th (East Anglian) Division, chosen after their storming of Umbrella Hill near Gaza.

The badges are identified in rows, from the top and left to right. *Top row:* 61st (South Midlands) Division, a cypher derived from the Roman letters for 61–L, X and I; 11th (Northern) Division, the *Ankus* or Egyptian key of life, chosen in that country; Russian Relief Force (white on blue), merely a distinctive sign. *2nd row:* 34th Division, chosen as a distinctive sign; 48th (South Midland) Division, a distinctive sign; 51st (Highland) Division, a cypher of H and D. *3rd row:* 67th (Home Counties) Division, a distinctive sign; 42nd (East Lancashire) Division, a red and white distinctive sign with an exhortation; 23rd Division, a distinctive Maltese Cross in a circle. *4th row:* 32nd Division, a cypher of four 8's (which make 32); XIX Corps, a pun (three 'whats' for its GOC, General Watts); the Cavalry Corps (St George is the patron saint of cavalrymen). *Bottom row:* First Army, a distinctive white stripe on all vehicles; 56th (London) Division, a 'territorial' sword from the arms of the City of London; 3rd Division, a yellow cross and circle from the arms of its GOC, General Haldane

French Motor Unit Insignia

From left to right, top to bottom: Section sanitaire 20, Section sanitaire 124, Commission regulatrice automobile Weil, Section sanitaire 17, Service telegraphique (Tenth Army), Section TM 431, Section sanitaire 141, Section sanitaire 625, Section TM 55, Section sanitaire 64, Section sanitaire 8, Section TM 716, Section TM 596, Section sanitaire 92, Section routiere 709, Section TM 48, Section TM 557 and Section TM273

Great Britain

Germany

United States of America

Italy

France

Rumania

Japan

Portugal

Greece

Austria-Hungary

Russia

Turkey

Although the navies of the First World War presented a drab sight in their grey basic paint schemes, the flags that each wore were entirely different. Usually, each navy had three types of flag, apart from signalling ones. First, normally worn on the jackstaff at the bows, was the jack (the national flag or a variation of it). The other two types, flown from masthead, yardarm or stern, were the naval ensign (the navy's flag) and the command flag of the officer commanding a fleet or squadron. *Left:* Ensigns of the First World War. *Right:* Dressed overall—the British fleet before the war. *Far right:* British naval flags. *Below:* HMS *Canopus,* flying all three main flags on her masts

NAVAL ENSIGNS

Great Britain

Ensign

Royal Standard

Jack

Admiral

Vice-Admiral

Rear-Admiral

Naval Reserve
Blue Ensign

Mercantile Ensign
Red Ensign

BLUE

YELLOW

RED

DHR

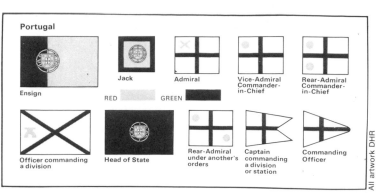

Portugal

Ensign

Jack

Admiral

Vice-Admiral Commander-in-Chief

Rear-Admiral Commander-in-Chief

RED   GREEN

Officer commanding a division

Head of State

Rear-Admiral under another's orders

Captain commanding a division or station

Commanding Officer

All artwork DHR

France

Ensign and Jack

Vice-Admiral

Rear-Admiral

Captain commanding a division

BLUE

RED

Naval flags and ships of some of the Allies are illustrated on this page. *Above:* The flags of the Portuguese Republican Navy and Merchant Marine. *Above right:* The flags of the French Navy. By arrangement, the conduct of the naval war against the Imperial German Navy in the North Sea and Channel was a British affair, the French Navy concentrating (not very efficiently) on the prosecution of the maritime war against the Austro-Hungarian Navy and German U-Boats in the Mediterranean Sea, in conjunction with the

Italian Navy and elements of the Royal Navy. *Immediately below:* Flags of the Greek Navy. *Below:* The flags worn by the third most powerful navy of the war — that of the United States of America. The Coast Guard Service (the Revenue and Life-saving Services combined) mounted anti-submarine patrols in the western Atlantic. *Bottom:* USS *New York*, flying three ensigns and a senior rear-admiral's flag (by the ensign at the head of the mainmast). *Right:* The 1903 French armoured cruiser *Ernest Renan*, wearing the jack at her bows

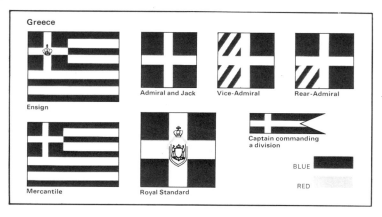

Greece

Ensign

Admiral and Jack

Vice-Admiral

Rear-Admiral

Mercantile

Royal Standard

Captain commanding a division

BLUE

RED

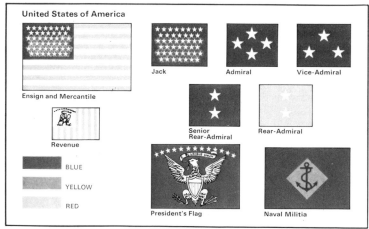

United States of America

Ensign and Mercantile

Jack

Admiral

Vice-Admiral

Revenue

Senior Rear-Admiral

Rear-Admiral

BLUE

YELLOW

RED

President's Flag

Naval Militia

Bibliotheque National

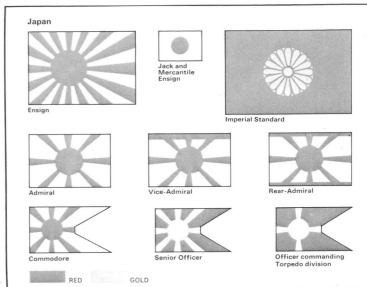

Japan

Ensign

Jack and Mercantile Ensign

Imperial Standard

Admiral

Vice-Admiral

Rear-Admiral

Commodore

Senior Officer

Officer commanding Torpedo division

RED   GOLD

Above left: The Japanese destroyer *Shirakumo* at the siege of Tsingtao in late 1914. The Japanese refused to send their fleet to aid the Allies in the Mediterranean, and restricted their naval activities to the siege of Tsingtao, pursuing the German East Asiatic Squadron out of the Pacific and escorting the Australian convoys at about the same time. *Above right:* Flags of the Imperial Japanese Navy

Left: The Russian dreadnought *Petropavlovsk.* She was built to a design originally drawn up by Cuniberti, the Italian co-father, with Fisher, of the dreadnought, but was completed so late that she was obsolete, with dreadnought armament and battle-cruiser protection. She is wearing the jack (based on the Cross of St Andrew, Russia's patron saint) at her bows. *Right:* The flags of the Russian Imperial Navy

Right, below centre: The naval flags of one of the smallest navies among the Allies, that of the soon-overrun Kingdom of Rumania. The largest ship in her navy was the 1,320-ton cruiser *Elizabetha,* mounting four 6-inch guns

Bottom left: The Italian submarine *Pullino,* flying the ensign from her stern. *Right:* Italy's naval flags. The Italian colours of red, white and green were the colours of Napoleon's Italian Legion in 1796. These colours were taken over about 50 years later by the King of Sardinia. To them he added the arms of his house, Savoy, a white cross on a red shield with a blue border. Victor Emmanuel, King of Sardinia, was proclaimed King of Italy in 1861, and his flag became the national one. The crown was peculiar to the navy

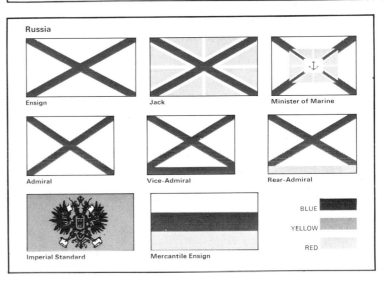

Russia

Ensign

Jack

Minister of Marine

Admiral

Vice-Admiral

Rear-Admiral

Imperial Standard

Mercantile Ensign

BLUE

YELLOW

RED

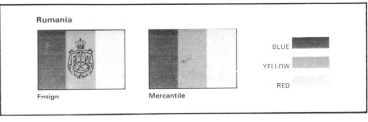

Rumania

Ensign

Mercantile

BLUE

YELLOW

RED

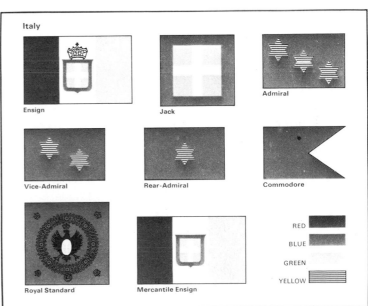

Italy

Ensign

Jack

Admiral

Vice-Admiral

Rear-Admiral

Commodore

Royal Standard

Mercantile Ensign

RED

BLUE

GREEN

YELLOW

Photograph above and right: Cousinly amity before the war: the 'Hohenzollern' gig carrying the Kaiser pulls away from the Russian Imperial yacht *Standart* in Swinemünde after a courtesy visit. The gig is flying the Imperial German Navy's ensign from her stern and a form of the Imperial Standard at the bows. The *Standart* is wearing the jack at the bows and flying the ensign from her stern. *Right:* Flags of the Imperial German Navy. The colours were derived from the red and white of the Hanseatic League and the black and white of Prussia. The black cross is taken from the arms

of the Teutonic Knights and the eagle from the arms of the rulers of Prussia, the Hohenzollerns. It was only after the war that the ensign became known as the 'Imperial War Flag'. *Below:* Turkish flags. Red is a traditional Moslem colour. The crescent was probably adopted from the badge of Constantinople, which the Turks took in 1453. The origin of the star is uncertain. The central motif in the Imperial Standard is the 'tughra', a symbol containing a stylised palm-print, the Sultan's name, the word *Khan* and a phrase meaning 'the ever victorious'.

Germany

Ensign

Jack

Grand-Admiral

Inspector-General of the Navy

Admiral

Vice-Admiral

Rear-Admiral

Commodore

Imperial Standard

Mercantile Ensign

Naval Reserve

BLACK

RED

Turkey

Ensign and Jack

Minister of Marine

Admiral of Fleet

Admiral

Vice-Admiral

Rear-Admiral

Commodore

Imperial Standard

RED

Right: The naval flags of the Imperial Navy of the Austro-Hungarian Empire. The colours of red, white and red were taken from the arms of Leopold Heldenthum, Duke of Beben-

berg, whose white coat became so bloodstained in a battle that the only white left was under his swordbelt. The eagle is that of the Habsburg family, the rulers of the Empire

Austria-Hungary

Ensign and Jack

Admiral

Vice-Admiral

Rear-Admiral

Commodore

Imperial Standard

Mercantile Ensign

BLACK

GREEN

YELLOW

RED

FRIEND OR FOE? NATIONAL AIRCRAFT MARKINGS

Despite the warnings of the prewar Hague Convention, which realised that national insignia on aircraft would be needed in any future war, Great Britain entered the First World War with no national markings, the only distinguishing marks being the army or navy serial numbers on the rudder. Though recognition sheets were issued to the infantry, the latter apparently took great delight in firing upon any aeroplane that flew within range of them, be it Allied or German. Such was the novelty of aeroplanes that untrained observers could not tell one from another. Thus the first initiative came from pilots, who took to painting Union Jacks on their machines in prominent positions. Late in August 1914, the Union Jacks were usually painted in the form of a shield; a directive sent out in October altered this to a full-chord standard-shaped emblem. The Union Jack framed by the outline of a shield was therefore abandoned. Another failing of this emblem as a national marking was that the St George Cross could be confused with the cross used by the Germans, so the RFC adopted the tricolour roundel used by the French air force, but with the colours reversed (red in the centre, blue on the outside). This took effect from December 11, 1914. The **BE 2a** illustrated shows the form of the roundel adopted initially by the RNAS, without a centre and with the red outermost. The RNAS soon took to the 'RFC roundel, however. The next problem to be faced by the RFC was that of camouflage. It was soon realised that aeroplanes could go about their business with much less disturbance if they blended with the colour of the ground, so that machines

above them would not notice them so easily. Although individual pilots had begun to experiment before the war, no general camouflage scheme was adopted by the British until late in 1916, when an upper-surface finish of brown/khaki-green (olive drab) was adopted, the under surfaces remaining the light shade of cream (plain-doped linen) the whole machine had presented before the era of pigmented dopes. Metal cowlings and the like were usually painted black or dark grey. Wooden parts were usually left in their natural colours. When night-flying aeroplanes started to appear, an all-over olive drab finish was adopted, with roundels minus the white portion. The **Sopwith Dolphin**, of 'B' Flight, 79 Squadron, illustrates a typical 1918 day camouflage and markings. The **SE 5** shows standard RFC and RAF fuselage camouflage and markings (note the rudder striping) and the special coloured additions of 60 Squadron in the summer of 1917. The High Command soon insisted that these non-standard markings be removed, as it did with all active service squadrons. The only machines to get away with bright finishes were those on Home Establishment.

The French, unlike the British, had realised the need for national markings as early as 1912. In that year they adopted the roundel (red circle outermost) based on the cockade of the Revolutionary era. This was placed in all the areas now considered normal, except for the fuselage sides. The rudder markings adopted were three vertical stripes of blue, white and red, with the blue stripe leading. When the British adopted the French markings and reversed the order of the colours on the roundels, they did not do so with the rudder stripes.

The French had much the same experience as the British with camouflage, but adopted a system of disguising their machines in late 1916/early 1917, when a green and buff upper-surface camouflage was chosen. The lower surfaces remained clear- or grey-doped. Night-flying aeroplanes were painted blue-black overall, upper and lower surfaces, and had only rudder stripings as national markings.

The aces, a term coined by the French, were allowed great latitude in the marking and finish of their machines, and several had very brightly coloured aeroplanes. Names were fairly common, as were unit insignia, and many aces

also painted a diagonal band round the fuselages of their aircraft, the band being made up of three thin stripes of red, white and blue.

French squadrons were numbered consecutively in order of formation, letters being prefixed to the number to indicate the type of aeroplane being flown by the unit. These letters were an abbreviation of the name of the manufacturer, V for Voisin, SAL for Salmson and so on. If a squadron changed the type of aircraft it flew, the prefix altered accordingly.

The **Nieuport 17** illustrates the upper-surface finish peculiar to SPADs and Nieuports in late 1916, before the introduction of camouflage. The **SPAD XIII** is in the standard green and brown/buff camouflage used from 1917 onwards. The machine is in the unit markings of *Escadrille* SPA 48. The **Breguet 14** is in the finish usual to bomber aircraft: buff overall, and is from *Escadrille* BR 127.

French naval aeroplanes started the war in natural finish, but were usually finished in grey overall from 1917 onwards. Instances of ordinary air force camouflage were not infrequent, however, especially on fighters, which might be co-operating with air force units. Late in the war, an anchor was added to the roundel to indicate that the aircraft on which it was painted was a naval one.

When Italy entered the war in May 1915, she altered her markings from the earlier pattern of individual squadron designations and aircraft serial numbers to the more common Allied practice of roundels and rudder striping. These were in the national colours of red, white and green. The peculiar aspect of the Italian system, however, was that the red and green circles were interchangeable in position, apparently at the whim of the unit. As there was no other country that used these colours, there was no risk of confusion.

Camouflage was not standard, but most squadrons seem to have devised their own particular patterns, some of them very garish. Much use was made of iridescent paints. The **Savoia-Verduzio-Ansaldo 5**, of the 87° *Squadriglia (La Serenissima),* illustrates Italian markings and colourings for smaller aircraft. Larger ones, such as the giant Caproni bombers, had the same national markings but were usually left in their natural, clear-doped finish. The 87° *Squadriglia,* incidentally, was

associated with the city of Venice, as the unit insignia (the Lion of St Mark, Venice's patron saint) and title indicate.

After Belgium had been over-run by the Germans in 1914, the Belgian air force was rebuilt by the French, with French equipment and machines. It played a small but important part in the war thereafter, and produced a celebrated balloon-busting ace in Willy Coppens de Houthulst.

Basic camouflage on Belgian aircraft, from the beginning of 1917 onwards, was an upper-surface finish of pale grey and green camouflage, with grey under surfaces. The French pattern of national markings was followed, with the Belgian colours of red, yellow and black replacing the French ones. This is illustrated on the **Hanriot HD 1,** a type used by the Belgians as one of their main fighters, despite the fact that it was a French design that had not found favour in its own country. It was also used in Italy in considerable numbers, and acquitted itself well in both areas.

The Imperial Russian air forces used a variety of different markings during the course of the war. The wings and fuselage were marked with a square and a triangle respectively, each divided into white, red and blue portions. There was an alternative to this, however, in the form of an optional roundel, with more rings than was usual on Allied aircraft (a white outer ring, then red, white, blue and white again in the centre). The Imperial Russian Navy also used a rudder marking in the form of the naval ensign—a blue St Andrew's Cross on a white background. The use of these markings was somewhat haphazard, some large aircraft, for example, having two roundels on the fin, one above the other. The Russians were also unusual in painting a roundel on each side of the tailplane on some types of aircraft.

At the beginning of the war, Russian aircraft were in natural doped finish, but by the beginning of 1915 a grey overall finish had been adopted as standard, and this remained the authorised colour until Russia dropped out of the war at the end of 1917.

The **SPAD A2** and **Morane-Saulnier L,** both French types in service with the Russians long after they had become obsolete on the Western Front, illustrate the somewhat odd appearance of Russian markings and overall finish.

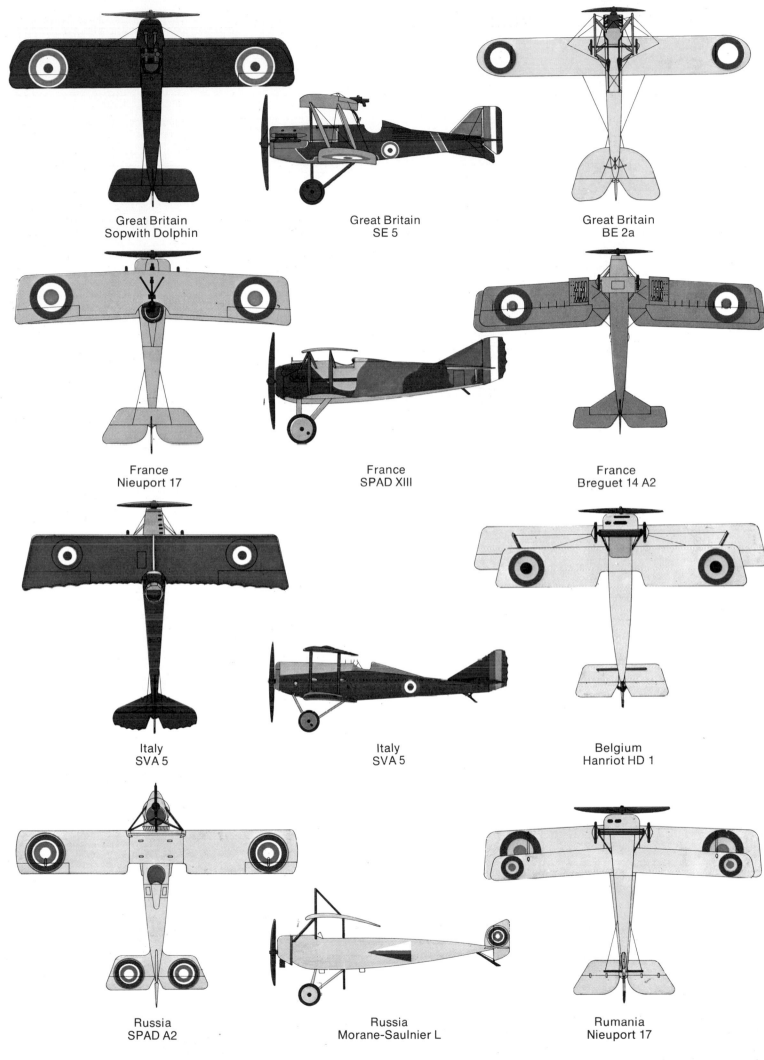

Great Britain
Sopwith Dolphin

Great Britain
SE 5

Great Britain
BE 2a

France
Nieuport 17

France
SPAD XIII

France
Breguet 14 A2

Italy
SVA 5

Italy
SVA 5

Belgium
Hanriot HD 1

Russia
SPAD A2

Russia
Morane-Saulnier L

Rumania
Nieuport 17

Rumania's small air force was equipped wholly with aeroplanes of French origin, and not surprisingly her national markings were derived from the French ones. As Rumania's colours were red, yellow and blue, however, the white of the French roundel was replaced by yellow in the Rumanian roundel. The **Nieuport 17** makes this difference apparent. The basic colour scheme for Rumanian aircraft was the same as that for Russian ones – pale grey overall.

Serbia's air force was equipped solely with French types, and the Greek air force almost entirely with them. The national colours of Serbia were the same as those of France, so identical markings were used. After her entry into the war, Greece's air force, which had been very weak in 1914, became ever stronger and more efficient, and also used French insignia on its machines. No Serbian or Greek machines are shown.

Japan's war effort in the air was restricted to gunnery and artillery spotting at the siege of Tsingtao in 1914. The majority of the aircraft used were French, although an increasing number of indigenous types made their debut during the course of the war. By 1918, several types of British machines were being adopted, and the illustration of Japanese markings is on a **Sopwith 1½-Strutter.**

Portugal's air force took no part in air operations on the Western Front, but did undertake war flights from the Azores, patrolling against German U-Boats. Her markings are illustrated on the **FBA Type B** flying boat. Portugal possessed a fair number of British and French flying boats.

China's minuscule air force took no part in the war, but as she was one of the Allies, her markings are shown here, on the **Caudron G III.**

The story of the markings used by the United States is a lengthy one. The need for national markings first became apparent during the Mexican-American 'war' of 1915. As a result, a blue star in a white disc was adopted as the marking for aircraft accompanying the US expedition. There was still no ruling on the markings for aircraft at home.

On arrival in France, the air units of the American Expeditionary Force adopted the by-now standard roundel of the other Allies, but with the order of the colours altered to avoid confusion with the roundels of the French and British air forces. These

were, from the outside, red, blue and white. The rudder stripes were red, white and blue, in that order from the rudder hinge. These markings were always made as large as possible, the wing roundels often extending from leading to trailing edge. Late in 1917, these AEF markings were adopted as standard in the US also.

Aircraft in the US were finished in a buff colour, while those destined for France were usually painted with a dope that produced a pale grey finish. The war experience of the Allies had shown camouflage to be vital, however, and the AEF's air units thus started to use a version of the French system, although very considerable latitude was allowed to the various squadrons.

The US Navy opted for different markings. On April 21, 1917 the Navy chose a variation on the earlier star-in-a-circle motif. This was a red-centred white star in a blue disc, while the rudder stripes were the same as the AEF. (In fact, it was the AEF which copied the stripes of the Navy.) In 1918, the Navy adopted the AEF roundel for its aircraft in the European theatre in place of the star, but the latter was retained for other areas. Before the war, the Navy's standard finish had been plain varnished fabric, but in mid-1917 a navy-green or navy-grey finish was adopted. The US Marine Corps' aeroplanes were in the same finish as the Navy's, and had similar markings, with the exception of the roundel on the fuselage side. This had an anchor across it. The **SPAD XIII,** of the 22nd Aero Squadron, shows the standard AEF markings, the **DH 4** those of the day-bomber squadrons and the **Thomas Morse Scout** those of the US Marine Corps' aircraft.

The Central Powers differed entirely from the Allies in the form of their national markings. They eschewed the roundel entirely, and based their markings on the square or portions of it, as in the square Turkish symbol and the cross of the other powers, with their straight outer edges. The idea behind this was not initially to make the markings of the Central Powers radically different from those of the Allies. It was more an opportune accident, based on the fact that the most obvious symbol for the Germans, the leaders of the Central Powers, was the cross of the Hohenzollern family of Prussia. Thereafter, it was

copied by the other Central Powers in form and in colour, and became a marking very different and distinct from that of the Allies.

The German national marking, then, was the Cross Pattée, or Iron Cross, from the arms of the royal house of Prussia. This was in use from the start of the war until the spring of 1918. On March 20, 1918 it was ordered that from April 15 of the same year the earlier type of cross should be replaced by the Greek Cross, known to the Germans as the *Balkankreuze*. And, unlike the Allies, the Germans used the same marking on the fin/rudder and the wings. Although the cross was basically just that – a black cross – it soon proved necessary to add a contrasting white edge to let the cross stand out against the background colour of the wing. (The difference between the Cross Pattée and the Greek Cross, incidentally, is this: the former's limbs are wider at their ends than in the centre, where they join, and do not have parallel sides, whereas the latter has straight and parallel sides.)

As with the other countries fighting in the First World War, camouflage was at first unknown in Germany. Up to the end of 1915, all aeroplanes had a natural cream or buff finish, the colour of doped linen, but this often became a dull grey when subjected to the outdoor rigours of active service. The first form of camouflage was introduced in 1916, when an experiment (in which natural fabric was overprinted with a screen of small black dots) was tried, with very little success. Later in the year, at about the time the Allies were coming to realise the need for camouflage, the Germans also introduced their own pattern, a sprayed-on colour scheme of green, purple and brown patches on all upper surfaces. Later, with the introduction of types with a rounded fuselage, it became possible to use an under-surface camouflage, in which a well-defined line could be established between the upper and lower surfaces. Where this was possible, the under surface was painted grey-blue. When paint became rare in 1918, these machines were left with their plain plywood fuselages merely varnished.

The deterioration of Germany's overall war situation meant that from late 1917 onwards, the German Empire had great difficulty in obtaining linen of good enough quality to cover aircraft. Even when this was obtainable, it could

not take the number of coats of dope to proof it and to camouflage it, and so camouflage-printed fabrics were introduced. These were of two types. For the smaller aircraft, there were fabrics with lozenge or irregular shaped patterns in black, blue, brown, green, yellow and pink. For larger machines, such as the G and R machines, there was a fabric with an 18-inch hexagon pattern of black, blue, grey, red-mauve, blue-mauve and sage green.

This latter type of fabric was of too inferior a quality for the wings and tailplanes of the large R types, so these lifting surfaces were covered with the best linen available, usually hand-painted to match the regular hexagons of the printed fabric used on the fuselage and fin/rudder units.

The **Albatros D III** (*Leutnant* Voss of *Jasta 5*) shows typical fighter camouflage and markings of the spring of 1917, the **Roland C II** (*Leutnant* Seibert of *Fl Abt 5*) the pilot's individual markings and the national markings of the autumn of 1916 and the **Pfalz D XII** the 1918 markings and camouflage of *Leutnant* Kammerer of *Jasta 35*. Although the national insignia were fixed, other markings were not, and great latitude was allowed to pilots in fighter units, especially the aces.

Austria-Hungary used the earlier German markings throughout the war, with the addition of three broad stripes of red and white (the latter in the middle) on the wingtips of naval aircraft, as a form of ensign. These markings were also carried on the tail occasionally, as on the **Phönix D I** fighter shown. Camouflage followed the German pattern.

Initially the Turks used an emblem based on their national flag, with a white crescent and star on a red square, but in 1915 they changed this to a white-edged black square. This was done to avoid confusion with the red on Allied markings and to bring the markings into conformity with the black and white of the other Central Powers. The Turks used German aircraft throughout the war (flown for the most part by Germans too), with a natural or sandy brown finish **(AEG C IV).**

Bulgaria's markings, like Austria-Hungary's, were the same as Germany's. The cross on the lower wing had no white edging **(Fokker E III).** On the upper surfaces, the Bulgarians used a strip of green paint along the trailing edge of the wing to differentiate their machines from German ones

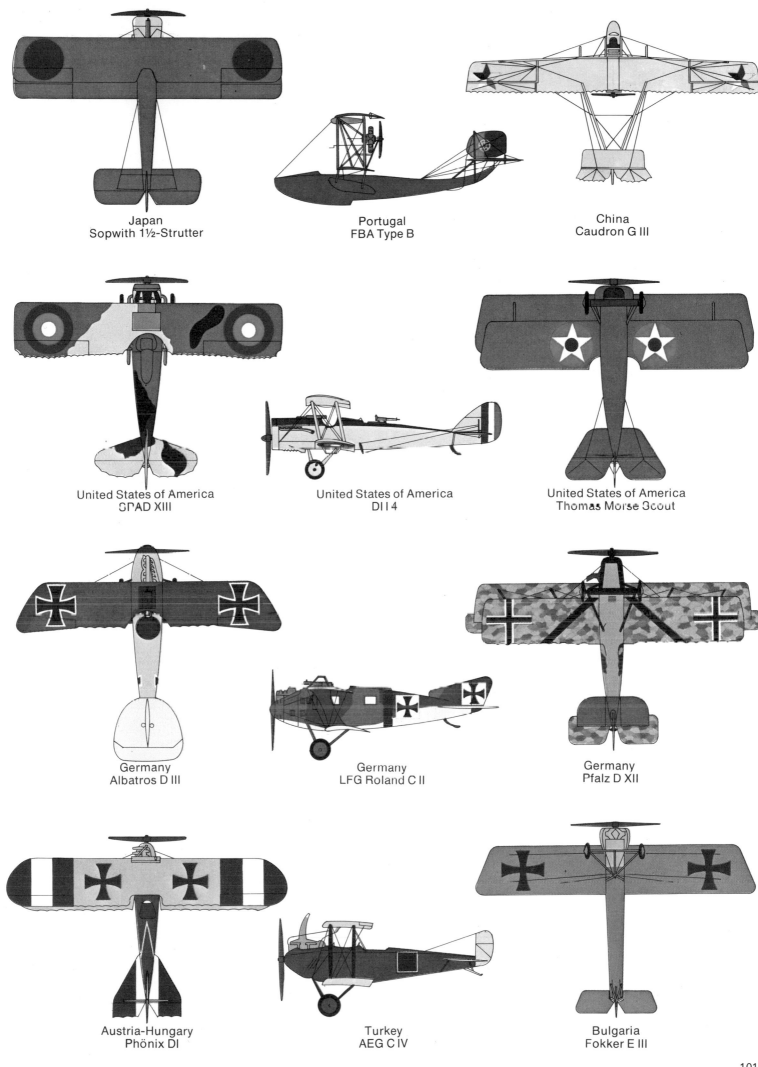

Japan
Sopwith 1½-Strutter

Portugal
FBA Type B

China
Caudron G III

United States of America
SPAD XIII

United States of America
DH 4

United States of America
Thomas Morse Scout

Germany
Albatros D III

Germany
LFG Roland C II

Germany
Pfalz D XII

Austria-Hungary
Phönix D I

Turkey
AEG C IV

Bulgaria
Fokker E III

THE ACES AND THE JOKERS INDIVIDUAL AIRCRAFT MARKINGS

Pilots are almost by nature individualists, and the First World War gave these men the opportunity to let their extrovert personalities have free rein. This took many forms: wild and riotous living, hair-raising stunt flying, a constant attempt to debunk authority, 'brass hats' in particular, and last but not least the extraordinary private markings of their aeroplanes. The Germans had a penchant for bright, regular patterns over large areas of their machines; the Russians for the macabre; the Italians for iridescent paint and fanciful animals; the French for names and animals; the British for overall gaudy paint schemes if they could get away with it; and the Americans for comic figures. This is necessarily oversimplified, for such a list can be neither exclusive nor comprehensive, but gives an idea of the sort of men who flew these early warplanes. Even if the exercise of this individualism did not stretch over the whole machine, most of the prominent pilots, with the exception of the British, managed to add small but distinctive personal and unit markings. *Left:* The real thing: two French markings. *Above:* The Sioux head unit marking of the *Escadrille* Lafayette, a volunteer unit of Americans flying with the French air force.

Far Left top: The unit marking of *Escadrille* SOP 226, a French unjt using British Sopwith 1½-Strutter reconnaissance aeroplanes, as the name of the unit and the binoculars around the chicken's neck indicate. *Far left centre above:* The unit marking of *Escadrille* SPA 6, a SPAD fighter unit. *Far left centre below:* Typical fighter unit emblem—the greyhound and hare of SPA 81. *Far left bottom:* The emblem of the US 91st Aero Squadron in France. *Photograph bottom of page.* The flaming comet personal markings of *Leutnant* Bertrab. The aircraft is an Albatros D III fighter. *Photograph, left above:* A prancing devil decorates the side of this Italian Pomilio PD general purpose machine. Note also the rear-view mirror at the left hand side of the cockpit. *Photograph, left below:* A marking that was to gain great fame in the next World War on the aircraft of the 'Flying Tigers'—the American Volunteer Group operating with the Chinese against the Japanese. Here the shark's mouth is under the nose of a British Sopwith Dolphin fighter in 1918. This is a very blatant marking for a British machine, and the pilot was no doubt soon told to remove it

Stato Maggiore Aeronautica

Bayer Hauptstaatsanchiv, Munchen

Unit markings of the First World War, usually on the fuselage sides.

Left, top to bottom:
The US 22nd Aero Squadron (SPAD XIII); the US 25th Aero Squadron (SE 5a); the stork of *Escadrille* SPA 73 (SPAD XIII), one of the squadrons making up the élite *Cicognes* (Storks) *Groupe,* France's premier fighter unit. Each *escadrille* used a different variation of the basic stork symbol. The US 95th Aero Squadron (Breguet 14 A2), a bomber unit.

Right, top to bottom:
The most famous American symbol — the 'Hat in the ring' of the 94th Aero Squadron (SPAD XIII and Nieuport 28). The symbol denoted the United States' final entry into the war. The Polish 16th Reconnaissance Squadron (Breguet 14 A2), operating against the Russians in 1920. The US 11th Bombardment Squadron (DH 4). The *cocotte* (a stylised bird made of folded paper) of *Escadrille* C 11 (Caudron G III).

Opposite page left, top to bottom: Large Union Jacks were painted on the wings and fuselages of British aircraft from late August 1914 to early 1915. They were easily confused with the German cross, however, and replaced by roundels. The aircraft are Bristol Scouts of the RNAS in France. A French SPAD single-seater. Another great French type, in this instance a Salmson 2 A2 two-seater reconnaissance aeroplane. The emblem neatly sums up what the observer must have felt when he stood to peer over the side! One of France's favourite sons, Georges Guynemer, in the dark uniform, with a general inspecting his SPAD *(Vieux Charles),* the beginning of which can just be seen to the left of the general's legs. Note also the *cicogne.*

Opposite page right, top to bottom: Fuselage roundel on US Marine Corps' aircraft. It was all red with the exception of the eagle's head and chest (white), the centre of the roundel (white) and the middle ring of the roundel (blue); the dragon sported on the side of his Albatros D V by *Leutnant* Hans Joachim von Hippel. The dragon was red, with yellow flames issuing from its mouth; the markings of *Escadrille* BR 127 (Breguet 14 A2 bombers); the duck family markings of the *Section Artillerie Lourde 220* (Breguet 14 A2) artillery reconnaissance unit; the US 147th Aero Squadron (Nieuport 28) with the motto (not painted on the aircraft) 'Who said rats'

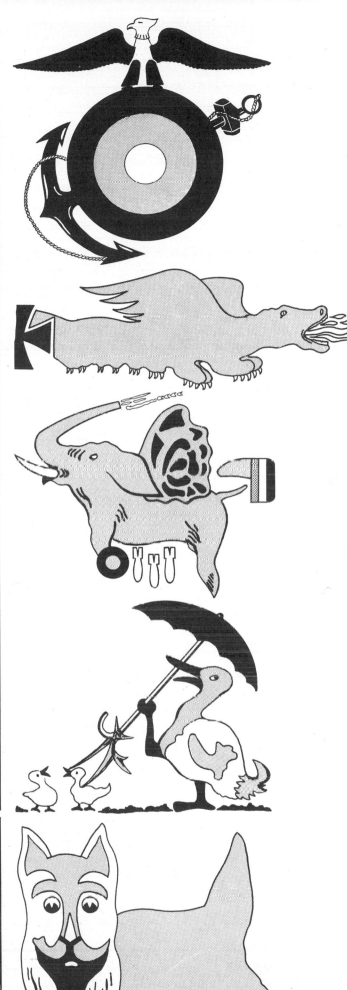

Uniforms of the Second World War

By the Second World War, uniforms had become almost totally functional, and the demands of camouflage were paramount. Yet, as the small selection below indicates, there was still much room for variety.

Most countries of the world adapted the British naval uniform to a design for their own. A seaman's rig was also worn by some Petty Officers, such as a gunner in charge of a crew in the turret of a destroyer: a Petty Officer in the First Class Gunnery Rate (QR1). It consisted of a blue square-necked blouse and bell-bottomed trousers, jumper, collar with three white stripes (which did *not* commemorate Nelson's three great battles), white cap with the ship's name on the band, and black shoes or sea boots. A QR1's insigne of crown above and below crossed guns was worn on the upper right sleeve; on his left sleeve he wore a crown above crossed anchors and probably a three-year service chevron below. On a destroyer he slept in a hammock and stored his gear in a locker. His simple, wholesome diet was predominantly stews, his nightly beverage cocoa; he was daily issued with $\frac{1}{8}$ pint of neat rum. He could have joined up at the age of 15 but after some boys were lost in early actions they were not allowed to go to sea until aged 16. Experienced men up to the age of 55 were recalled for active duty in wartime. He could have done his gunnery course at Devonport or one of several other training centres. His pay was 5/6 a day plus family allowances.

RAF: Fighter Pilot, Pilot Officer

British Army: Lance-Corporal

The British soldier was recruited into an old regiment or the territorial militia; young men volunteered or were called up as a matter of course. A rifleman was given a thorough military training with accent on physical fitness and use of equipment. His rifle, a .303 Lee-Enfield No. 4 with cruciform bayonet and weighing 8 lb 10$\frac{1}{2}$ oz, or a No. 1 with sword bayonet and weighing 4 oz more, held 10 rounds in the magazine and could fire up to 15 rounds per minute. Riflemen also carried 60-round Bren gun magazines in their pouches and 1$\frac{1}{2}$ lb grenades which they could hurl up to 30 yards. They paraded and marched in ranks of three, dressed in waist-length battle jackets with two patch pockets, trousers with a large and small pocket on the front, and a forage cap, all wool-khaki. In action he carried a small personal pack, blanket, ground sheet, rations, helmet and gas mask, leaving greatcoat and spare clothing stored at the rear. His shoulder straps, belt, and gaiters were of webbing. Regimental or corps insignia were worn on his cap, cloth insigne of division on his left sleeve, over the rifle-green distinguishing mark, also in cloth. His daily pay was 2/9; after two years' service it rose to 3/6. Promotion to Lance-Corporal added 6d a day.

Royal Navy: QR1, Petty Officer

A Pilot Officer, lowest commissioned rank in the RAF, began training as an Aircraftsman II at an initial training school and first flew on his two-month elementary course, soloing after about seven hours' instruction in a TigerMoth. After another four months, on Proctors, he qualified for his wings and commission (pilots graduating as Sergeants were usually commissioned during squadron service), then went to an operational training unit to fly fighters with experienced instructors. Altogether he would have spent over a year in training and up to 200 hours in the air as well as 'blind flying' time in a Link trainer. His minimum age was 18, maximum 35; average height was 5 ft 8$\frac{1}{2}$ in. He had passed a written entrance examination, a physical examination, and a colour blindness test. He wore either a serge woollen blue-grey uniform or a four patch-pocket barathea with blue shirt, black tie, and black shoes. His rank insigne was a 'half-narrow' blue and grey ring around both sleeves; his wings were white-drab silk with a crown over the RAF monogram and brown silk laurel wreath. In the tropics he wore cotton khaki. The badge on his peaked cloth cap was a gold crown eagle and laurel wreaths. He was paid 11/- a day, plus £25 a year flying pay and dependents allowance.

A 2nd Lieutenant pilot in the USAAF was the highest paid of the five junior officer pilots illustrated here: he received $150 a month plus 50% flying pay and dependents allowance. His training courses, which were a series lasting nine weeks each (until 1944, when they were extended to 10 weeks) began at a pre-flight school, followed by the three-stage flying training system—Primary, Basic, and Advanced. In primary, he flew 60 hours in a Stearman or a Fairchild, then in a Vultee BT-13 in basic, and qualified for his wings and commission after his advanced course in a North American TT-6 (Harvard). He then went to a transition training centre where he flew combat planes; he gained altogether over 200 hours, and many Link trainer hours, during a training period which lasted well over a year. His standard of living was high, although he sometimes had to exist on army hard rations. Age limits were 18 and 35. His pilot's insigne was a US shield in the centre of metal wings, worn on the left breast, and his rank a single silver gold bar worn on epaulettes; his service arm insigne, a vertical silver propeller and wings, was worn on both lapels under two lots of brass US letters. He wore light or dark olive-drab uniforms; in the tropics he wore cotton khaki with rank and service arm insignia worn on shirt collars. His cap was leather peaked and its badge the USAAF eagle.

US Army Air Force: Pilot, 2nd Lieutenant

US Army: Private First Class

A Private First Class (PFC) in the US Army was a collar-and-tie soldier in his service uniform of olive-drab and wore solid brass US letters on one lapel, crossed rifles insignia on the other. His PFC chevron, on a blue background, was worn on the upper part of both sleeves; if he had qualified as a sharpshooter he wore the award badge on his left breast. His pay was $54 a month and $56.70 after 3 years and, in 1944, an extra $10 for Expert (training, conduct) or $5 for Combat (conduct in action). An infantryman's average height, in 1943, was about 5 ft. 8 in. His draft age was lowered, in 1942, from 20 to 18. A 17-week training programme was designed to teach him courtesy, discipline, the Articles of War, sanitation, hygiene, first aid, guard duty, PT, equipment handling, tent pitching, and he was given at least two weeks of continuous field exercises under simulated battle conditions with live ammunition adding to the realism. He wore web gaiters over his well-designed boots, clothing suitable for various climates. He carried a rolled poncho quarter-tent, blanket, pack, water bottle, gas mask, ammunition on a web belt, and a trenching tool. His rifle was either a .30 semi-automatic M1 (5.2 lb 15-round magazine, knife bayonet) or an M 1903 A3 (short or long bayonet). His hand grenade was a Mark II TNT 'pineapple'.

US Navy: Gunner's Mate, Second Class

A Gunner's Mate, Second Class, in the US Navy was a Petty Officer; on an aircraft-carrier he could be in charge of the crew serving a 5-in. gun which, because it 'could do anything but shoot straight down', was also an anti-aircraft gun. He could have trained at San Diego, having joined the Navy at 18. At the top of the sleeve of his blues or whites he wore two chevrons under crossed cannon and an eagle. He was issued with a blue cap with his ship's name lettered on its ribbon, but he more often wore the plain white turned up 'gob' cap. If his gunnery team had excelled at practice he would have worn an 'E' on the sleeve of his blouse; he also wore a striped collar and bell-bottomed trousers, or wore sea boots over work dungarees. During his early training (when ordinary seamen received $21 a month) he was taught to swim. On a carrier, in 1942, he was paid $60 a month for his rank, plus family allowances, and lived very well with as many as six items for breakfast, eight for dinner, and eight for supper. He could buy Coca-Cola and had the facilities of a library and a cinema; but there was no hard liquor on board.

Red Air Force:
Fighter Pilot

A Russian fighter pilot would have had the benefit of sound flying training before the war began but the experienced men were shot out of the skies in the first few weeks of the German attack: even later, when there *were* trained pilots available, there were too few aircraft left to fly. As the supply of fighters increased, young men over the age of 18 were given a hurried instruction on a primary trainer, possibly a YAK-3, and advanced training on a YAK-9 which was also in combat use. As aircraft supply, and losses, increased, training was more and more shortened and during 1943-44 many pilots went to their squadrons with as few as eight or ten hours' experience on a YAK-9. At times he could not be paid. Based behind the lines he fared better than the troops did on their rations. If he survived, despite his lack of training he was quickly promoted ; some generals were in their early 30s. His uniform style was that of the Red Army—jerkin buttoned at collar and cuffs, breeches, black Sam Browne belt and field boots, and his cap was either a forage or peaked. Gold stars studded his blue collar insignia. He wore a TT 7.62-mm automatic pistol.

Red Army:
Private First Class

A Red Army soldier was brought up to habits of obedience at home and as a cadet. He joined at the age of 18 and was on the reserve until the age of 45 ; in 1944 boys of 14 and 15, and men of 70, were called up for non-combatant duties. He was often a fatalist,and naturally resourceful. His khaki uniform was the same as his officers' and he was well equipped for winter with felt-lined field boots and a long warm greatcoat. A Private First Class was paid 95 kopeks a day although often he received no pay at all and back-pay was written off. His dependents, however, were regularly remunerated. Promotion was rapid, as there was a high proportion of officers of many grades in a battalion : in fact, a section could be commanded by a lieutenant of the third grade. Political indoctrination, security, and censorship in a regiment was controlled by a group headed by a major. If the regiment, or division, distinguished itself it was awarded the title 'Guards' and pay was doubled. A soldier captured unwounded was regarded as a deserter. His bayoneted rifle, the M-1930 7.62 mm, weighed about 9 lb and its magazine held five rounds. His submachine-gun, the PPSH 7.62 mm, fired 71 rounds from its drum magazine. His standard grenade was the 'stick' variety.

Red Navy:
Gunner, Petty Officer

With four old battleships and no carriers and only a few cruisers and some 30 destroyers forming the heavy part of the Red Navy fleet, most recruits were sent to serve on one of the numerous submarines or motor torpedo-boats based in the Black Sea, the Pacific, or the Baltic Sea, which is connected by canals with the Arctic Ocean. A Gunner's training in the Navy was of a higher standard than a soldier's and there was no necessity for the Navy to rely on the use of raw recruits. Serving a gun on a Russian submarine would be similar to the procedures used on a German submarine as the same type was used by the Red Navy. With 68,000 miles of navigable waterways in the Soviet Union, motor torpedo-boats were sometimes involved in actions inland, carrying supplies and ammunition, fighting off air attacks with twin-mounted machine-guns. Depending on the sector where he was based, paydays were unpredictable. For Baltic and Arctic conditions his uniform was well furred and lined to keep out the sub-zero cold. His temperate climate blues were cut in a German Kriegsmarine style, his cap was also similar and trailed the two ends of the cap-band ribbon. His badge was the hammer and sickle on a red star.

A *Gefreiter*—Private First Class—in the Waffen-SS (Schutzstaffel) was a member of an 'elite' corps based on racial purity and a high physical standard, and considered different enough to be a fourth arm of the German services. Because of a high casualty rate some late recruits were accepted from 'Germanic' countries. A German *Gefreiter* was paid 1.31 Reichsmarks a day. Recruits, aged 18 to 40, were highly trained, particularly in mobile warfare, and were intensely indoctrinated in politics. They ate, with their fork-spoon combination, as well as their excellent field kitchens could provide from rations or commandeered supplies. After four months of active service a *Gefreiter* could be promoted to NCO rank. In field dress he wore no unit insignia, his SS runes were on the right of his collar and helmet and national emblem on his upper left sleeve. He wore a green-grey uniform and three-quarter-length black boots with studded soles, and carried a quarter tent-cape, blanket, combat pack, tent rope, gas mask, canteen, entrenching tool, bayonet, haversack for personal items, and cartridge pouches containing 60 rounds of 7.92 rimless. His rifle, a Gewehr 98, weighed 9 lb, held a five-round magazine; his MP-40 machine pistol held 32 rounds. Grenades were either 'stick' or 'egg'.

German Army: SS Private First Class

German Air Force: Fighter Pilot, 2nd Lieutenant

A German 2nd Lieutenant fighter pilot began training at an elementary flying training school which entailed gliding on Course 1, elementary flying on Course 2, and single-engine fighter training on Course 3. He then went on to advanced training and lastly to his operational training unit: altogether it took seven to eight months and 107 to 112 hours at the controls. He wore the national eagle emblem on his right and pilot's insigne on his lower left breast. On his visored cap, more rakish than others in the army, was the national rosette flanked by oak leaves and spreading wings surmounted by a flying eagle. Yellow piping and a large 'W' decorated his epaulettes; his collar patch was an eagle and oak leaves on a yellow background. He wore jackboots, grey-blue wool-rayon breeches, jacket with patch pockets, grey shirt, black tie, and a Sam Browne belt with eagle-emblem buckle. His flying suit had zippered, slash pockets and his flying boots were lined. He had passed a rigid physical examination and was eligible for pilot training after the age of 18. Under normal conditions, Luftwaffe pilots enjoyed better food than the rest of the army and their pay was higher.

German Navy: Gunner

A German Navy Gunner could have enlisted when he was 16; most surface vessel seamen were enlisted before the war. He was trained under strict disciplinarians and was highly efficient, many gunners being awarded a *fourragere*, with a gunner's grenade attached to its end, for marksmanship. His uniform was dark blue (white in summer), the eagle-swastika national emblem worn over his right breast, three white stripes on his collar, Melton-cloth jumper with trousers, and black boots or sea boots. His blue rimless cap carried the name of his ship on a ribbon band which trailed two ends to the rear; an eagle and rosette in gilt were fixed above the band. His port or starboard division and watch were denoted by the number of stripes on his left or right arm. As a Gunlayer T (for turret) on a *Deutschland*-class pocket-battleship he wore a chevron surmounted by a T-marked grenade; for three years' service he would wear a second chevron. He was not provided with a greatcoat but wore a thick blue pea jacket with two rows of brass buttons. He slept in a hammock. His diet included a high proportion of dried fish and he sometimes received a rum issue. His pay was 1.61 Reichsmarks a day.

The Japanese soldier was given rigorous physical training and intense morale-strengthening discipline indoctrination; he was strong, agile, and loyal, preferring death to capture. Aged between 19 and 45, he was classified 'A' if at least 5 ft tall, 'B' if slightly under 5 ft and in good condition. Average height was 5 ft 3 in. A private's three gradings would include a year as First Class before promotion to Superior Private (10.50 yen a month); two years after enlistment he could qualify for Lance-Corporal's rank. Rice with soya sauce, dried fish, pickled plums, canned beef or whale meat, and dehydrated vegetables formed his staple diet of $2\frac{1}{2}$ to 4 lb a day. In the tropics he wore khaki cotton twill, puttees, hobnail or rubber-cleated boots, or split-toe sneakers. His blanket was more rayon than wool but his small tent was waterproof. His woollen cap was stitched with a gold star; his rank (three gold stars on a red patch) and unit insignia were worn on collar and sleeve. He wore a good-luck sash under his uniform and carried a pack (a canvas hold-all wrapped in his overcoat and tent-section), a trench tool, mess tin, water bottle, gas mask, and leather ammunition pouches on his belt. The metal of his helmet was of poor quality. His rifle was either the 6.5-mm ($9\frac{1}{4}$ lb) or 7.7-mm ($8\frac{1}{2}$ lb) with sword bayonet. Hand grenades were either Model 91 or 97 fragmentation, or else 'stick' high-explosive or incendiary.

Japanese Army: Superior Private

Japanese Army Air Force: Fighter Pilot, 2nd Lieutenant

A Japanese 2nd Lieutenant fighter pilot would have had an opportunity to have flown first in a glider at his high school or university. He could begin his Army apprenticeship between the ages of 16 and 18 (as young as 14 in 1943) as an Army Youth Soldier. Inducted into the Army, he began his initial flying training, which originally lasted 10 months but was reduced to three months in 1944. Pilots chosen to fly fighters went to an advanced flying school and then to an operational training unit. Until 1944, it took about 12 months before he flew on operations; very few at this stage were up to the general flying standard of British or American pilots. His flying suit was made of brown silk and cotton, water- and flame-proofed; his calf-length lined boots and helmet were of leather. He preferred not to wear a parachute; he carried a sword on parade, a pistol when flying. His field dress consisted of a button-up jacket, cap, and semi-breeches of greenish khaki. His rank of one star on a red and yellow striped patch was worn on the collar, his service insigne patch on his right breast. He wore heelless socks, cotton and wool underwear, and a soldier's red sash of 1,000 good-luck stitches. Promotion from the ranks was rare but a 2nd Lieutenant could advance by as much as two grades for meritorious service. Pay was 70.83 yen a month.

Whites and blues were also traditional colours for Japanese Navy uniforms, and seamen wore square collars and trousers more baggy than bell-bottomed. A Petty Officer Second Class in blues wore a peaked cap with a badge of yellow rope-encircled-anchor on blue. Five brass buttons closed his high jacket; he wore black boots; the collar rim of a white shirt showed under his jacket. His rank insignia was a bar over a carnation flower over an anchor surrounded by a wreath; these were in yellow on his upper right sleeve. On his left sleeve he wore the yellow flower emblem of the navy. Under normal conditions he would have taken five years to reach this rank. On an aircraft-carrier he could be the PO in charge of an anti-aircraft gun and its crew. His obedience and loyalty began in childhood—it was a common factor in his community; ancestor worship and belief in the divine origin of his Emperor and race increased his potential bravery in action. His constant training and strict discipline made him a highly efficient cog, irreplaceable when high casualties made sudden demands on manpower. His diet on board a carrier was much the same as the Army man's but with less fresh meat and vegetables, except when at training stations on the Inland Sea. His pay was 23 yen a month; (in 1941, 1 yen = 23 US cents or 1/2 Sterling).

Japanese Navy: Petty Officer, Second Class

Drawings/Julian Allen   Research/John Vader

THE ITALIAN SOLDIER

The Italian soldier's uniform was grey-green. Trousers were tucked into puttees, and the matching tunic was worn over shirt and tie. In the desert he was issued with a khaki tropical uniform, pith helmet, and tinted glasses. His rectangular identity plate was hung round his neck, listing his name, number, religion, date of birth, town, and province. With his arms, which could be one of a number of different kinds of rifle, he carried a bandolier of ammunition, an entrenching tool, and his water bottle. He was issued with a minimum of clothing, but was adequately fed, and received a wine ration when it was available. At Bardia the Australians were amazed to find bottles of scent in disused Italian dugouts

THE AUSTRALIAN SOLDIER

The Australian army uniform varied from greatcoat, jerkin, drab khaki jacket, and trousers, gaiters, brown boots and helmet (winter at Bardia), to shorts and boots, hatless, shirtless, and sockless (resting behind the lines at Tobruk). Green cotton shirts and trousers, US Army gaiters, boots, and slouch hat were worn in New Guinea. The hat was worn with the brim turned down except on ceremonial occasions when the left side was turned up. The badge of the AIF was worn on the collar dogs, and in a larger form on the turned-up hat brim. The badge was a semi-circle of swords and bayonets suggesting the rays of the sun, with 'Australian Military Forces' enscrolled underneath. The word 'Australia' also appeared on the shoulder epaulettes

THE NEW ZEALAND SOLDIER

Normally the New Zealand soldier wore the British Army uniform of khaki 'battle dress' and black boots. This was varied however to suit the climate of the theatre of operations. His broad brimmed hat, called a 'Lemon Squeezer' because of its shape, was usually worn when a helmet was unnecessary. In peacetime the NZ Army issued different badges for each district regiment but during the war the soldiers wore a universal insignia on the front of their hat puggarees: fern leaves rising to a crown, the letters NZ in the middle, and the word 'Onward' at the base. Also their country's name was woven into the cloth of their epaulettes. Here he carries a Lee Enfield rifle, and wears the same webbing equipment as the British Army.

Julian Allen

◁ A Royal Marine Commando.
Specialists in combined
operations, they were
used for such tasks as raids
on coastal emplacements

The men who fought for Burma

Gurkha soldiers have always been enlisted by private treaty between the British Commonwealth and the King of Nepal, and enjoy one of the highest fighting reputations of any of the native-enlisted units in the British Commonwealth and Empire armies. The national weapon—the *kukri* chopping-knife, with its deadly, razor-sharp half-moon blade—supplemented the standard British infantry weapons (Lee-Enfield rifle and Bren- and Sten-guns) in the Burma campaign. In the long retreat from Burma, the Gurkhas especially distinguished themselves in the battle for the Sittang river-crossing—and in the general tenacity of their performance in action, which was to add to their battle-honours in the years which lay ahead

An Allied assessment of the Japanese soldier (in a wartime manual) stated that: 'he meticulously performs duties allotted to him; he is an efficient cog in the machine, and will carry out instructions to the letter.' This tendency had inherent virtues and vices—but it did not impede the Japanese 'Runaway Victory' in the Pacific. His equipment was sound, but the Model 99 (1939) 7·7-mm rifle (and the 1905 Model 6·5-mm) had a magazine capacity of only five rounds as opposed to the British ten rounds. This slowed down the rate of fire—and the standard Model 92 machine-gun ammunition could not be used in the Model 99 rifle in the same way as the British Bren-gun and Lee-Enfield rifle

The British infantryman in Malaya and Burma was painfully learning the technique of jungle warfare from the Japanese, but his equipment was not inferior. Indeed, it gave far more attention to the comfort of the individual soldier than was to be found in the Japanese army system. The standard British rifle was the legendary Lee-Enfield Mk III, which had so high a rate of fire that the Germans at Mons in 1914 had mistaken it for machine-gun fire; the ammunition-pouches carried by the British infantryman held 60 rounds each—and the ·303-inch ammunition was the same as that fired by the Bren light machine-gun

Deirdre Amsden

117

US Marine Raiders: Commandos of the Pacific

The US Marine Raiders were trained to live and fight in a variety of conditions and circumstances. Their course included close-quarter fighting, demolition, sniping, and signalling. The seaborne equivalent of paratroops, they spearheaded attacks or raided enemy-held islands

Peter Fluck

National Archives

US Marine Corps

Top left: David Stirling, creator of the SAS, the greatest 'irregular' of the war. *Below:* Recruited from the experts on desert navigation, the Long Range Desert Group was constituted as a reconnaissance force, and as a means of striking a blow at bases in the enemy's rear. Mounted in open trucks armed with Lewis, Vickers, Browning, Breda machine-guns, Boys anti-tank rifles, or a Bofors gun, columns of the LRDG would often undertake desert journeys of thousands of miles

The British steel helmet, like the French one, remained basically unchanged in both world wars. The design—to protect the wearer from fire from above—can be traced back to the type of helmet worn at Agincourt, in 1415

The German helmet of the Second World War is clearly descended from that of the First World War, although the design is more functional and is far less flared

Early pattern Russian helmets show traces of French design in the vestige of a crest, and German design in the neck protection. This particular helmet was captured by the Germans

The Italian helmet of the Second World War was a design of the early 1930s, when Italian rearmament began. To improve the morale of the Italian troops, Mussolini thought that they should wear smarter equipment—and this helmet design matched the idea

The German paratroop helmet was designed to protect the head from the impact of landing, as well as from hostile fire. It was rounded, and the projecting flared edge was removed

The French used the same type of helmet in both world wars. The influence of tradition can be seen in the crest, badge, and decoration on what should be a functional design

The Japanese army and navy wore helmets of the same design, the navy having an anchor, the army a star. The sharply-sloping design seems to continue that of the samurai pattern, without the crest or the flange at the back

In the First World War the Americans wore the British-style helmet, but it was criticised for not protecting the neck. They then quickly developed a helmet incorporating this feature, with a padded lining for comfort

HATS AND HELMETS OF THE WAR

Luftwaffe officer's summer cap. The design is typically German; the normal colour for the upper part of the cap was blue-grey; in keeping with the more casual attitude of the Luftwaffe the sides of the cap have been bent down

The German army officer's cap shows the same design as that of the Luftwaffe, but without the informal sloppiness of the latter, which would not be tolerated in the army

The tank corps beret worn by Panzer crews in the early stages of the war had no particular function other than to enhance the prestige of the élite *Panzertruppen*. A leather helmet was worn inside the beret

The glengarry, worn by several Scottish regiments of the British army. Similar in some respects to the forage cap worn in both the army and the RAF, it was first adopted towards the end of the 19th century

The US army cap is again very similar in design to the glengarry and the British forage cap, although it is worn spread out more on the head, often with an aggressive rake

The cloth cap worn by the Japanese army was cheap and easy to produce, and was comfortable in tropical fighting. It is in fact very similar to that worn by American troops in postwar fighting in the Far East

The Royal Navy's basic cap design was worn by the crews of ships manned by sailors from Axis-occupied countries—such as Poland, as shown here. In summer the cap had a white cover

The cap worn by officers in the Women's Royal Naval Service is a descendant of the tricorn hat of the 17th Century, brought up to date and made to look more elegant

1. The Fleet Air Arm tie combines the Royal Navy colours with a broad light blue stripe

2. The tie of the RAF medical arm shows the RAF wings over the *caduceus* (the wand of healing) of the medical profession

3. United States Marine Corps. The Americans did not produce the same proliferation of ties as their British counterparts, and most US ties were for larger formations

4. In the Royal Navy, individual ships would produce ties. This is the tie of HMS *Sheba*

5. The RAF Volunteer Reserve, the RAF equivalent of the RNVR, has the same colours as the RAF but in a different pattern

6. Captured officers of the 51st Highland Division, to the amazement of their German guards, whiled away captivity devising the 'Reel of the 51st'

7. The minesweeping arm of the Royal Navy

8. The Brigade of Gurkhas. All Gurkha regiments were rifle regiments (black and green) but the 2nd Goorkhas wore red facings, hence the red stripe

9. The RAF

1. The tie of the 8th Army, the famous desert army which fought through North Africa to Sicily and Italy
2. The 14th Army, which achieved spectacular success against the Japanese in Burma

3. The tie of the Combined Operations staff, a mark of successful co-operation in 'Combined Ops', which was one of the most important achievements of the war
4. The Royal Armoured Corps included the Royal Tank Regiment as well as other former cavalry and infantry regiments

5. The Royal Army Medical Corps. One medical officer from this unit was attached to each battalion-sized unit.
6. The Parachute Brigade. The maroon background is the same as their famous 'Red Berets'

7. The Brigade of Guards tie reflects just that tone of discreet distinction that one expects from the sovereign's personal bodyguard
8. The Royal Marines, now adapted to a Commando role, are in fact 'naval soldiers'
9. The Royal Navy

Ties loaned by C. H. Munday Ltd.

POP ART OF THE AIR WAR

Both the Luftwaffe and the US Army and Navy air forces displayed more colourful insignia unit and personal on their aircraft than the air forces of the other combatant nations. The unit badges of the Luftwaffe were usually a monogram showing an emblem such as a heart or an ace of spades, or a design showing the function of the unit. Personal insignia were frowned upon, but those that were carried were usually of a gaudy colour scheme. The unit badges of squadrons of the air forces of the US normally featured subjects that were comic, or macabre. The glamorous insignia which are probably the best known of the US markings are personal badges painted on the aircraft by its crew, independently of the unit badge. These glamorous insignia correspond to the Luftwaffe's gaudy colours, though they show the crew's character more than the Luftwaffe's. *Above:* The unit badge of the 25th Bombardment Squadron is that of the 25th Squadron in the First World War in 1917, the notches in the axe of the executioner varying according to the number of aircraft shot down by the pilot while serving with the British Royal Flying Corps. *Top right:* The badge of VO-3. The designation shows this to be a naval squadron, the 'V' showing it to be an aircraft rather than an airship squadron, the 'O' an observation squadron, as is confirmed by the binoculars. *Right:* The insignia on the aircraft is an unofficial one, not submitted for approval at the time the photograph was taken in the Aleutians. *Far right:* Aircraft heraldic experts examining a design. The design under consideration has as its centrepiece 'Bomby-the-Bear', a character who appeared in the badges of the 470th to 473rd Bombardment Squadrons

Allan Rees

US Air Force

THE FLYING TIGERS

In 1937, a retired US Army Air Corps officer, Claire Chennault, became Chiang Kai-shek's adviser on aeronautical matters. His first force of Chinese and mercenary pilots proved unable to wrest air control from the Japanese, and during 1941 Chennault persuaded Chiang to allow him to recruit pilots in the United States—to fly and fight at $600 a month plus $500 a kill. This American Volunteer Group soon became known as the 'Flying Tigers' from its distinctive emblem and, using the efficient early-warning system which Chennault had been able to build up, quickly established air supremacy over the Japanese. In 1942, after America had officially entered the war against Japan, the Flying Tigers were disbanded and a China Air Task Force set up under Chennault.

Flying Tigers scramble to meet a Japanese attack. *(Right)* Crewmen rearm a Tomahawk during a lull between missions. *(Below)* The famous Flying Tiger symbol. *(Below right)* Claire Chennault, apostle of omnipotent airpower

MEDALS OF THE SECOND WORLD WAR

British Victoria Cross
US Legion of Merit

US Congressional Medal of Honour (Navy)
Japanese Order of the Rising Sun
German Knight's Cross with Oak Leaves & Swords

French *Croix de Guerre* with Bronze Palm
British George Cross

Medals by courtesy of Spink & Son, Ltd., and the Imperial War Museum

FOR COURAGE ON LAND, SEA, AND AIR

Medals by courtesy of Spink & Son, Ltd., and the Imperial War Museum

1. **British Distinguished Service Order:** for commissioned officers' 'distinguished services under fire'.

2. **British Distinguished Flying Cross:** for 'acts of courage, valour, or devotion to duty performed while flying on active operations by officers and warrant officers'.

3. **US Distinguished Flying Cross:** for enlisted men and officers distinguished by 'heroism or extraordinary achievement while participating in an aerial flight'.

4. **US Purple Heart:** for all personnel killed or wounded in combat.

5. **US Silver Star:** for gallantry in action not warranting the Medal of Honour or DSM.

6. **Soviet Order of the Red Star:** for 'conspicuous services in the defence of the USSR in war or peace'.

7. **US Distinguished Service Medal (Navy):** for 'exceptionally meritorious service to the government in a duty of great responsibility'.

8. **US Distinguished Service Medal (Army).**

9. **British Military Cross (MC):** officers' award 'for gallant and distinguished service in action'.

10. **British George Medal:** awarded when circumstances are not so outstanding as to merit the award of the George Cross.

11. **French *Medaille Militaire*:** for officers and NCOs who specially distinguish themselves in war.

12. **British Military Medal:** for bravery in the field by NCOs and other ranks.

FOR KEY CAMPAIGNS AND WAR SERVICE

1. **1939/45 Star:** for service in operations between September 3, 1939, and August 15, 1945. Qualification period: six months' operational service
2. **Atlantic Star:** for service in the Battle of the Atlantic, on convoys, their escorts, in anti-submarine forces, and unescorted fast merchant ships. Qualification: six months' operational service
3. **Air Crew Europe Star:** for operational flying from UK bases over Europe (including the UK). Qualification: two months' operational service

4. **Africa Star:** for entry into all operational area in North Africa between June 10, 1940, and May 12, 1943, including service in Abyssinia, Somaliland, Eritrea, and Malta
5. **Pacific Star:** for operational service in the Pacific theatre of war, including naval and RAF personnel
6. **Burma Star:** for operational service in the Burma theatre as from December 11, 1940
7. **Italy Star:** for service in the Aegean, Italy, the Dodecanese, Greece, Sardinia, Sicily, and Yugoslavia, between June 11, 1943, and May 8, 1945

8. **France and Germany Star:** for operational service in France, Belgium, Holland, or Germany between June 6, 1944, and May 8, 1945
9. **Defence Medal:** for three years' service in the UK between September 3, 1939, and May 8, 1945; overseas until August 15, 1945. It could be awarded in addition to other campaign stars
10. **War Medal:** for full-time personnel of the British armed forces, irrespective of place of service, for 28 days' operational or non-operational service

SHIELDS AND MEDALS FOR SERVICE ELSEWHERE...

1. German shield for the 1943 Kuban campaign
2. German shield for service in the Far North
3. French Resistance medal
4. US medal for service in the ETO (European Theatre of Operations)
5. German shield for the Battle of Demyansk,

when a large German pocket was successfully supplied by airlift
6 and 7. German Iron Cross, Second Class, with bar for subsequent awards
8. German medal for troops engaged in the 1941-42 winter campaign in Russia

9. German shield for the Crimean campaign, 1941-42
10. German shield for the Battle of Narvik, 1940
11. Polish Army Active Service Medal
12. Medal for troops of the Fighting French

Medals by courtesy of Spink & Son Ltd. and the Imperial War Museum

AND A SELECTION OF NOT-SO-FAMOUS MEDALS

1. Soviet medal for distinguished services in battle
2. Soviet medal for the 250th anniversary of Leningrad
3. Dutch Nazi Party award
4. French Combatant's Cross
5. Medal for the Spanish 'Blue Division'

on the Eastern Front
6. Soviet Order of the Patriotic War, Second Class
7. British Disabled Serviceman's Badge
8. British Air Raid Precautions Badge
9. German War Service Cross in Bronze
10. German/Italian North African medal

(prematurely struck for the Axis entry into Cairo)
11. German Mother's Cross in Bronze (for bearing four to five children)
12. German medal for Indian troops of the *Azad Hind* (Indians serving with the Wehrmacht for a 'Free India')

Medals by courtesy of Spink & Son Ltd and the Imperial War Museum

From the beginning, the war in Russia was proclaimed by Stalin to be a patriotic war, and the spirit of 'Mother Russia' was duly invoked to inspire the troops of the Red Army. With traditional nationalism supplementing international Communism as Russia's inspiration, medals and orders for valour based on the nationalist motif began to appear. Below are four examples. *Left to right:* The 'Order of Admiral Nakhimov', the 'Order of Suvorov', the 'Order of Alexander Nevsky', and the 'Order of Kutuzov'. All were pre-revolutionary heroes of Russian history; Kutuzov, for example, was the general who hounded Napoleon's troops out of Russia after the burning of Moscow in 1812

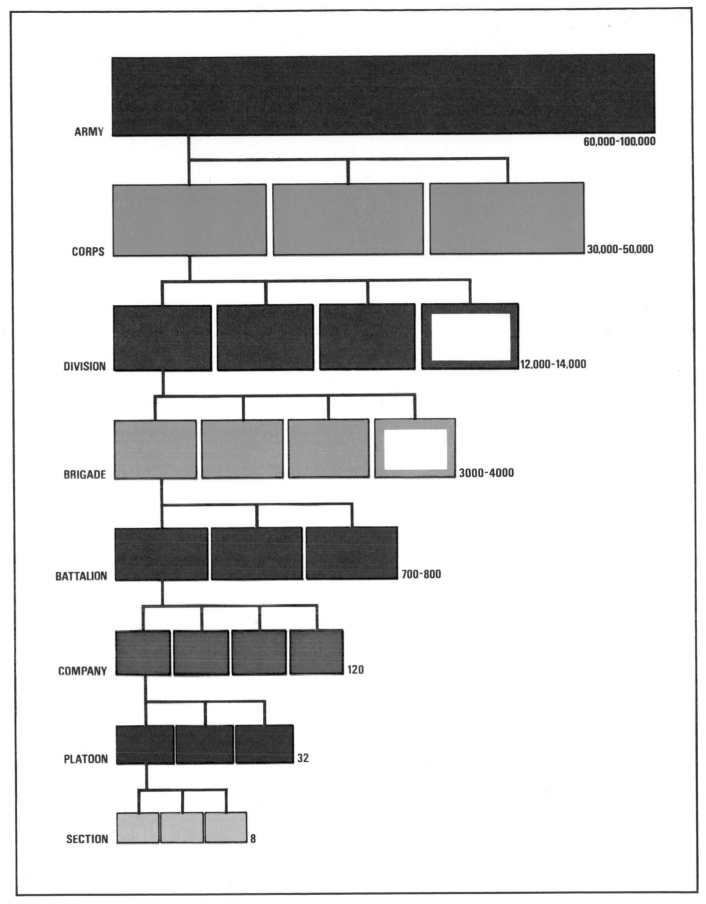

ARMY 60,000-100,000

CORPS 30,000-50,000

DIVISION 12,000-14,000

BRIGADE 3000-4000

BATTALION 700-800

COMPANY 120

PLATOON 32

SECTION 8

BREAKDOWN OF AN ARMY

This chart shows the breakdown of the basic components of a British army, from the infantry section upwards. Supporting arms and headquarter formations have been omitted, but their numbers have been included in the strength estimates. From brigade level up the strengths vary enormously. A division could have more or less than three brigades, a corps several divisions, and an army several corps, depending on the tasks to be carried out. The hollow boxes indicate the probability of a further unit in that formation. By the end of the war there was a tendency to form mixed groups out of different units. For instance an infantry brigade might borrow an armoured regiment for support, and an armoured brigade an infantry battalion. Further support could be gathered from higher formations. In the British army for example, the Royal Artillery, the Royal Engineers, the Royal Signals, and many other support services had units attached to all formations. The total strength of each formation, then, is greater than the sum of its basic components.

Throughout the Second World War, the infantry units of the main combatants were organised along basically similar lines. Three major formations at each level were the core around which the supporting arms and services were collected. The difference in size between the US and British divisions can be explained by the American practice of holding more supply, maintenance, and heavier artillery units at Corps or Army level, and allocating them to the divisions for specific operations. The British division was more self-contained. In practice, both infantry divisions, with extra supporting troops and services, employed about 42,000 men (only 5,000 of whom were riflemen on the ground)

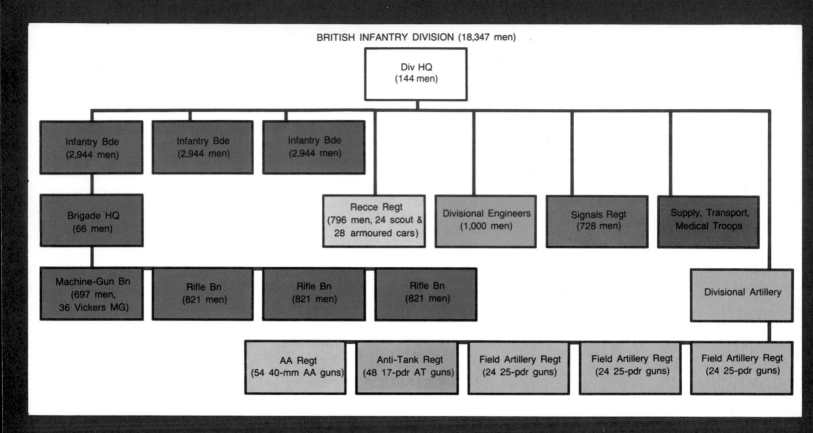

BRITISH INFANTRY DIVISION (18,347 men)

Div HQ (144 men)

Infantry Bde (2,944 men) · Infantry Bde (2,944 men) · Infantry Bde (2,944 men)

Recce Regt (796 men, 24 scout & 28 armoured cars) · Divisional Engineers (1,000 men) · Signals Regt (728 men) · Supply, Transport, Medical Troops

Brigade HQ (66 men)

Divisional Artillery

Machine-Gun Bn (697 men, 36 Vickers MG) · Rifle Bn (821 men) · Rifle Bn (821 men) · Rifle Bn (821 men)

AA Regt (54 40-mm AA guns) · Anti-Tank Regt (48 17-pdr AT guns) · Field Artillery Regt (24 25-pdr guns) · Field Artillery Regt (24 25-pdr guns) · Field Artillery Regt (24 25-pdr guns)

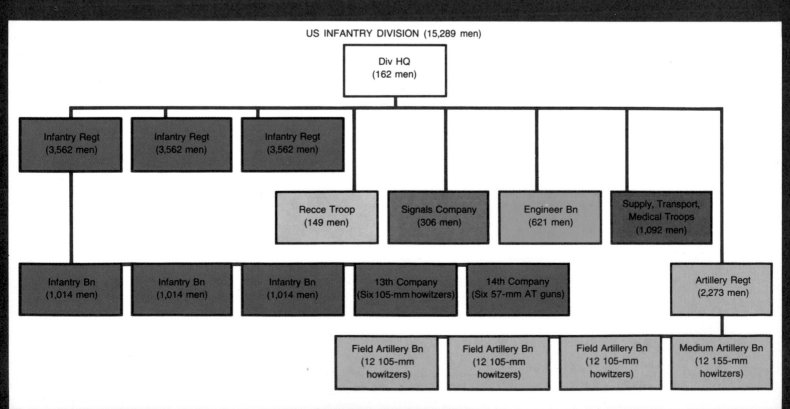

US INFANTRY DIVISION (15,289 men)

Div HQ (162 men)

Infantry Regt (3,562 men) · Infantry Regt (3,562 men) · Infantry Regt (3,562 men)

Recce Troop (149 men) · Signals Company (306 men) · Engineer Bn (621 men) · Supply, Transport, Medical Troops (1,092 men)

Infantry Bn (1,014 men) · Infantry Bn (1,014 men) · Infantry Bn (1,014 men) · 13th Company (Six 105-mm howitzers) · 14th Company (Six 57-mm AT guns)

Artillery Regt (2,273 men)

Field Artillery Bn (12 105-mm howitzers) · Field Artillery Bn (12 105-mm howitzers) · Field Artillery Bn (12 105-mm howitzers) · Medium Artillery Bn (12 155-mm howitzers)

The organisation of armoured divisions was far more flexible than that of the infantry. The British method tended to be somewhat rigid during the early stages of the Normandy campaign, with combat units assigned to the two main brigades, and the mixture of armour and infantry going no lower in the scale; whereas the Americans used a highly flexible system, with all combat units being held by the division, and assigned for a particular operation to either Combat Command A or Combat Command B. In this way, a combat team would be tailored to the particular type of fighting it could expect. The charts on these two pages show the approximate strengths of the main units in typical divisions

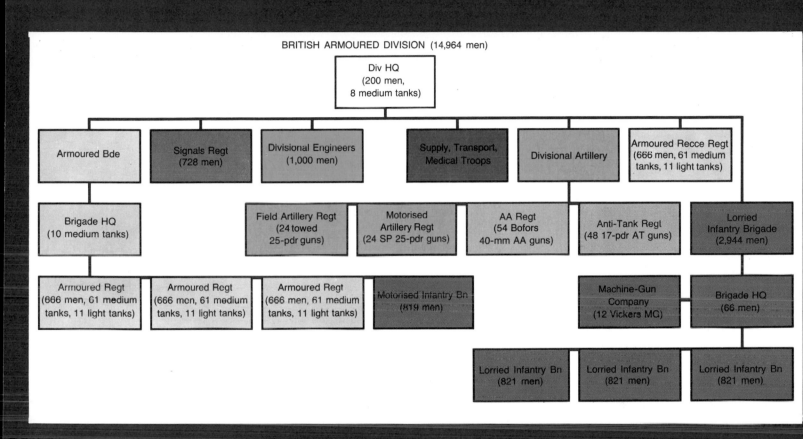

BRITISH ARMOURED DIVISION (14,964 men)

Div HQ
(200 men,
8 medium tanks)

Armoured Bde

Signals Regt
(728 men)

Divisional Engineers
(1,000 men)

Supply, Transport,
Medical Troops

Divisional Artillery

Armoured Recce Regt
(666 men, 61 medium
tanks, 11 light tanks)

Brigade HQ
(10 medium tanks)

Field Artillery Regt
(24 towed
25-pdr guns)

Motorised
Artillery Regt
(24 SP 25-pdr guns)

AA Regt
(54 Bofors
40-mm AA guns)

Anti-Tank Regt
(48 17-pdr AT guns)

Lorried
Infantry Brigade
(2,944 men)

Armoured Regt
(666 men, 61 medium
tanks, 11 light tanks)

Armoured Regt
(666 men, 61 medium
tanks, 11 light tanks)

Armoured Regt
(666 men, 61 medium
tanks, 11 light tanks)

Motorised Infantry Bn
(819 men)

Machine-Gun
Company
(12 Vickers MG)

Brigade HQ
(66 men)

Lorried Infantry Bn
(821 men)

Lorried Infantry Bn
(821 men)

Lorried Infantry Bn
(821 men)

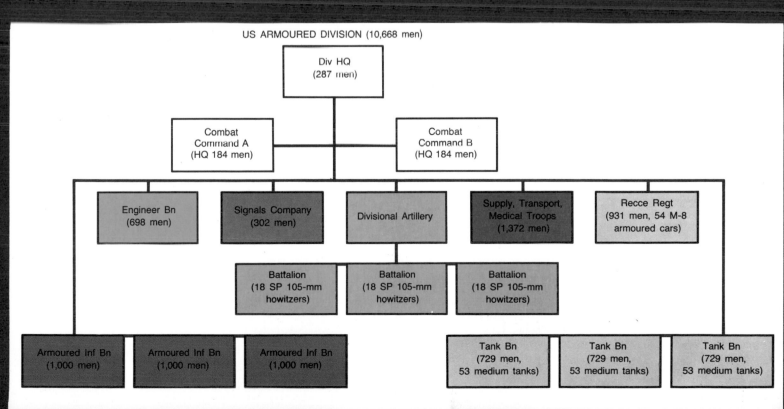

US ARMOURED DIVISION (10,668 men)

Div HQ
(287 men)

Combat
Command A
(HQ 184 men)

Combat
Command B
(HQ 184 men)

Engineer Bn
(698 men)

Signals Company
(302 men)

Divisional Artillery

Supply, Transport,
Medical Troops
(1,372 men)

Recce Regt
(931 men, 54 M-8
armoured cars)

Battalion
(18 SP 105-mm
howitzers)

Battalion
(18 SP 105-mm
howitzers)

Battalion
(18 SP 105-mm
howitzers)

Armoured Inf Bn
(1,000 men)

Armoured Inf Bn
(1,000 men)

Armoured Inf Bn
(1,000 men)

Tank Bn
(729 men,
53 medium tanks)

Tank Bn
(729 men,
53 medium tanks)

Tank Bn
(729 men,
53 medium tanks)

FIGHTING UNITS ON THE EASTERN FRONT

Although they differed greatly in size, the German and Russian infantry divisions used the same basic 'triangular' structure—although by 1944 the Germans had withdrawn one of the three infantry battalions in a regiment, but given the remainder heavier weapons. Both divisions were well supplied with their own artillery although the Germans tended to integrate theirs at a lower level, while the Russians had provided a powerful mortar element within the infantry regiment. Neither nation adhered strictly to the establishments which were laid down, and the charts on these pages only show typical divisional strengths on the Eastern Front during the latter stages of the war

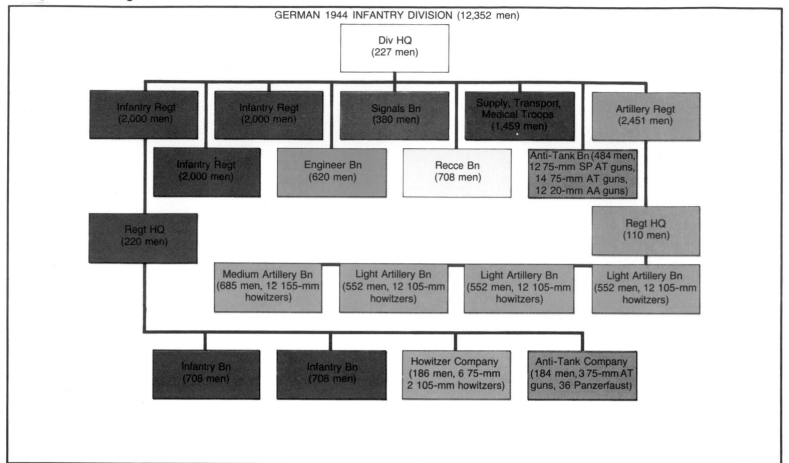

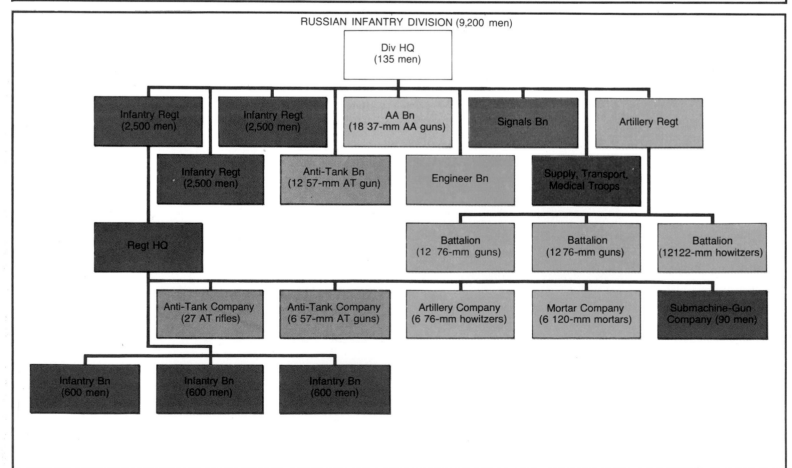

The organisations of the German Panzer division and its Russian equivalent the armoured corps were basically different. Although the early Panzer divisions had equal proportions of infantry and armour—two three-battalion regiments of each—the number of tanks had been progressively reduced so that by 1944 there were often only two armoured battalions—usually capable of providing less than 70 combat-ready tanks—with four Panzer Grenadier battalions. The Russian corps was well-balanced—with the equivalent of three western tank battalions (the three brigades) to three infantry battalions and a lavish scale of support weapons including a Katyusha rocket-launcher battalion

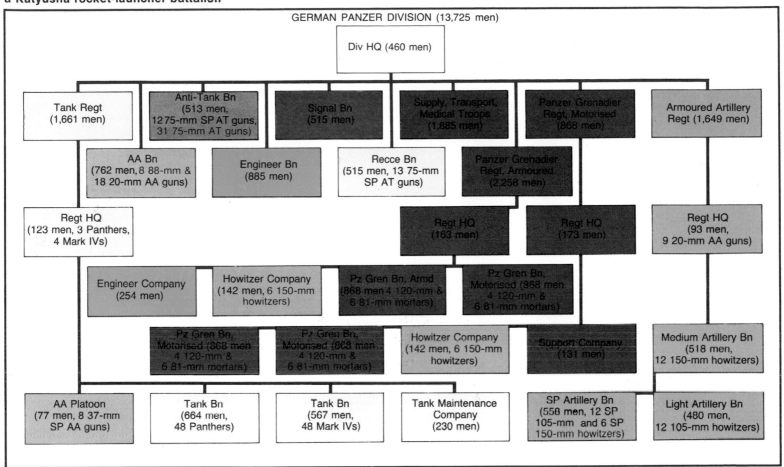

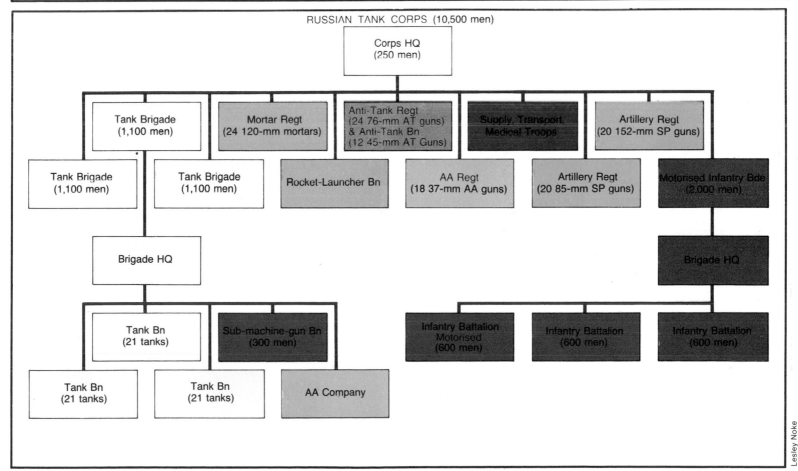

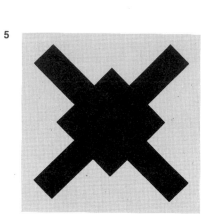

The 49th (West Riding) Division first saw active service in Norway, but in May 1940 the division was sent to form the main part of the occupation forces when Iceland was occupied. Previously the badge of the division had been the white rose of Yorkshire, but the emblem of a polar bear looking down into the water of the Atlantic was adopted when the first units arrived. Later the badge was taken up by the British troops in the island. The styling of the polar bear was

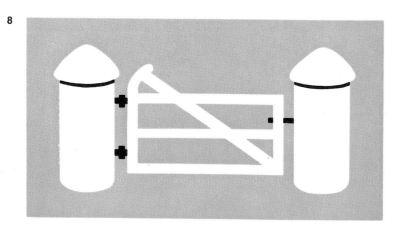

BADGES AND FLASHES FOR ALL ECHELONS

1. The badge of Malta Command. Like all formation badges of units on the island, it showed the Maltese Cross on the formation's colours
2. The 1st Corps' Engineers featured on their badge the spearhead of 1st Corps and the colours of the Royal Engineers
3. After the Norwegian campaign of 1940, a Viking ship was chosen as the corps badge to commemorate this service
4. The 8th Anti-Aircraft Division's badge shows an enemy aircraft crashing as a result of anti-aircraft fire
5. The 18th Division, a second-line Territorial unit. The badge is a stylised windmill, denoting the East Anglian origins of its units
6. The 27th Armoured Brigade, which formed part of 21st Army Group with the British Liberation Army in North-West Europe
7. The shield of St Oswald of Northumbria marks the badge of the Northumbrian District of Northern Command (and the local Home Guard)
8. The Northern Ireland District badge shows a gate typical of those found in the area

2

3

1

then changed to one looking up-wards, head up in defiance. In 1943, the division returned to the United Kingdom and became one of the units earmarked for the invasion of Europe. It formed part of the 21st Army Group, and landed in Normandy in June 1944, from then on taking part in operations in France, Belgium, and Southern Holland. The 49th Division ended the war under the command of the Canadian 1st Army, liberating the Netherlands.

4

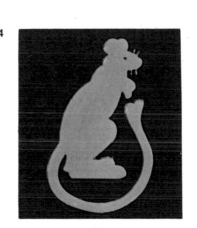

5

6

7

8

Allan Rees

1. The badge worn by the units of REME (Royal Electrical and Mechanical Engineers) serving in Southern Command. All units in this Command had the 'Southern Cross' on their badge
2. HQ Staff, South-East Asia Command: the phoenix of Allied might rising from the ashes of Japanese conquest
3. The 77th Division's badge, showing Excalibur, King Arthur's sword, indicates the division's West Country origins
4. The 'Desert Rats' – the 7th Armoured Division – adopted the desert jerboa as its emblem
5. The 72nd Independent Infantry Brigade
6. The Guards Armoured Division adopted the badge designed by Major Sir Eric Avery which the Guards Division made famous in the First World War. The Guards Armoured Division was formed in 1941
7. The garrison of the Orkney and Shetland Islands ('Osdef') took the naval 'Foul anchor' as its emblem because of its association with the Home Fleet base at Scapa Flow
8. The badge of the 2nd Division features part of the coat of arms of the Archbishop of York

141

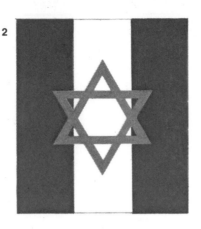

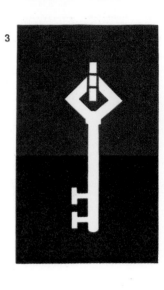

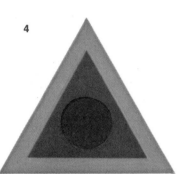

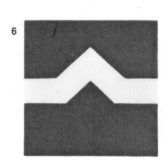

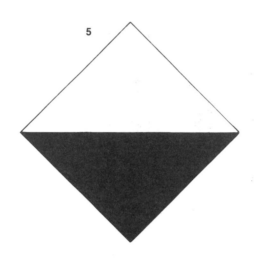

1. The 3rd Indian Division (Wingate's 'Chindits') took a gold Burmese dragon as its symbol
2. The badge of the Jewish Brigade Group which was formed in Palestine and served in Europe. Shows a Star of David on the postwar Israeli colours of blue and white
3. A key, showing that Gibraltar was the key to the Mediterranean, appeared on the badge of all units of the Gibraltar garrison. This is the badge of the 18th Defence Regiment, Royal Artillery. (The background colours are those of the Royal Artillery)
4. Many badges were based merely on geometrical forms; this example is the badge of the 2/2nd Casualty Clearing Station of the Royal Army Medical Corps
5. Another of the geometrically-based smaller formation badges. This specimen was worn by the 2/24th battalion of some infantry regiments
6. The badge of the 6th Fortress Company
7. The 31st Indian (Armoured) Division was formed in Iraq and served there and in Persia, Syria, and Egypt. In late 1945 it was renamed 1st Indian Armoured Division and returned to India in 1946
8. After the Allied takeover of Iraq, Syria, and Persia, the 10th Army, under General Sir Henry Maitland Wilson, adopted this badge for the Persia and Iraq Command
9. The HQ of East African Expeditionary Force had as its badge a rhinoceros, an animal symbolic of East Africa

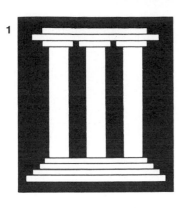

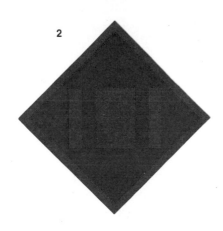

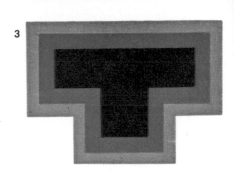

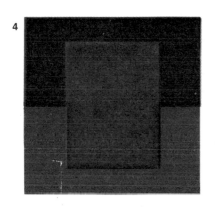

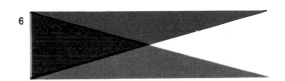

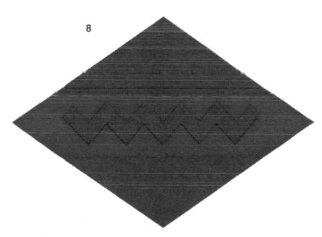

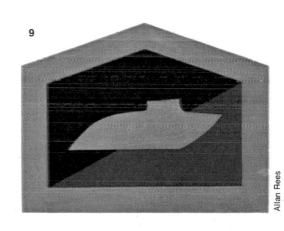

Allan Rees

1. The badge of No 3 District, Central Mediterranean Force, shows the three pillars of the temple of Castor and Pollux in Rome, forming the Roman numeral III for No 3 District
2. The Royal Engineers' Depôt, whose badge this is, was at Chatham at the beginning of the war, moving in 1941 to the prewar barracks of the Duke of Wellington's Regiment in Halifax, Yorkshire. The badge was worn by the permanent staff of the depôt

3. An alternative to the 2/24th Infantry Battalion badge (opposite page, No 5)
4. The badge of the Torres Strait Light Infantry Battalion
5. This badge was worn by the HQ Staff of the British 13/25th Brigade
6. The pennant of the Polish 1st Anti-Tank Regiment
7. The badge of the Australian Division incorporates two well-known Australian symbols.

The division left Australia in January 1940 for the Mediterranean theatre, fought in the Western Desert, Greece, Crete, and Syria; it was then transferred to the Far Eastern theatre and saw action in New Guinea
8. The zigzag central line in the badge of the Canadian 1st Army Group Royal Artillery is similar to that of the tie of the Royal Artillery
9. The badge of the Australian 2/7th Armoured Regiment features a First World War tank

1. **The King's Own Royal Regiment (Lancaster).** raised in 1680; granted its badge by William III and its title by George I

2. **Lincolnshire Regiment.** Raised in 1685 by James II; received its title in 1881, and became a 'Royal' regiment in 1946

3. **The Queen's Royal Regiment (West Surrey);** raised in 1661 to garrison Tangier, part of the dowry of Charles II's queen

4. **Royal Army Chaplains' Department (Christian).** The motto 'In This Sign Conquer' is attributed to Constantine the Great

5. **The Berkshire Yeomanry** has as its badge the White Horse of Uffington, a prehistoric landmark on the Berkshire Downs

6. **Royal Regiment of Artillery:** formed in 1716 under the old Board of Ordnance, whose arms included three cannons

7. **The 11th Hussars (Prince Albert's Own):** raised as dragoons in 1715, becoming hussars in 1840 after escorting Prince Albert on his way to marry Queen Victoria

8. **The 14th County of London Regiment (London Scottish):** raised in 1859 from Scotsmen living in London

9. **Royal Warwickshire Regiment:** raised in 1673 for Dutch service, coming onto the English establishment in 1688

10. **Lovat Scouts,** raised in the Boer War; crest and motto are those of the Clan Fraser, of which Lord Lovat was chieftain

11. **Australian Commonwealth Military Forces:** worn by all Australian personnel

12. **Royal Armoured Corps,** formed in 1939 from the Royal Tank Corps and mechanised cavalry regiments

SMALL SELECTION

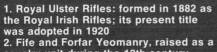

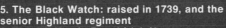

1. **Royal Ulster Rifles:** formed in 1882 as the Royal Irish Rifles; its present title was adopted in 1920

2. **Fife and Forfar Yeomanry,** raised as a cavalry unit during the 19th century

3. **The 17/21st Lancers;** the 17th was raised in 1759, the 21st in 1861. The badge, that of the 17th, was chosen in memory of Wolfe, killed at Quebec in 1759

4. **Royal West African Frontier Force:** composed of West African units: first battle honour came in the 1873-74 Ashanti War

5. **The Black Watch:** raised in 1739, and the senior Highland regiment

6. **The 8th King's Royal Irish Hussars:** raised in 1693 as dragoons, becoming hussars in 1822

7. **Corps of Military Police.** In 1855 12 NCOs from cavalry units formed the first mounted MPs; in 1885 the Military Foot Police was formed. They were united in 1926

8. **The 5th Royal Inniskilling Dragoon Guards;** raised in 1685 as a regiment of horse, becoming dragoon guards in 1788

9. **3rd 'The King's Own' Hussars:** raised in 1685, becoming 'King's Own' in 1714 and hussars in 1861

10. **The Tank Corps** was formed in 1917; the motto was granted in 1922; it became the Royal Tank Regiment in 1939

11. **Parachute Regiment:** formed in 1942 as part of the Army Air Corps, it received its own badge in 1943

12. **Grenadier Guards:** received the title after defeating the grenadiers of Napoleon's Imperial Guard at Waterloo

THE BRUTAL REICH

'The art of propaganda consists precisely in being able to awaken the imagination of the people through an appeal to their feelings, in finding the true psychological form that arrests the attention and appeals to the heart of the nation's masses'

Thus Hitler summed up his approach to propaganda in *Mein Kampf*. And in the swastika, unmistakable symbol of the Third Reich, he found his 'true psychological form'. *Below:* Mass mesmerism in action: the Führer addresses a crowd of SS and SA men, more than 100,000 strong, at one of the great pre-war Nazi rallies. The effectiveness of the Nazi heraldry in unifying a whole nation and rousing it to militaristic frenzy is a staggering reminder of the power mere symbols, skilfully used, can exert to hold ostensibly rational men and women to an ideal — even when that ideal is almost unthinkably evil.

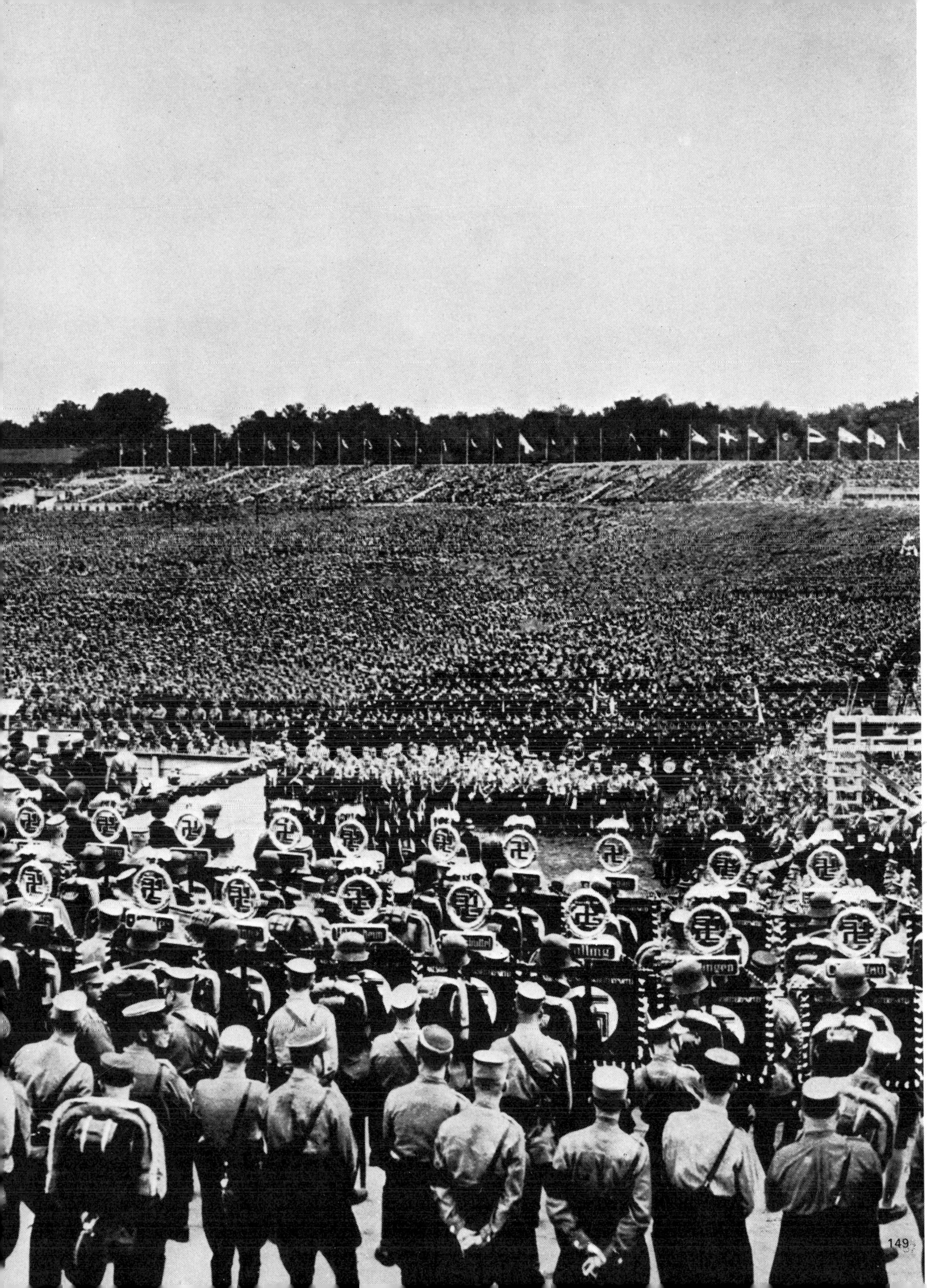

HIMMLER'S ARMY

Meine Ehre Heisst Treue – 'Loyalty is my honour' – the motto of the 'asphalt soldiers' of the Waffen-SS. Conceived as a bodyguard, transformed first into a police élite and then into a military shock force, it came eventually to serve only itself, on terms which made a mockery of the racial principles which had guided its growth. And in the end it betrayed its 'honour' by treachery. Aptly symbolised by their death's-head badges, the three elements of Himmler's SS – the Waffen-SS divisions, the Gestapo, and the concentration camp guards – have come come to stand for all that was most chilling in Hitler's Germany.

The illustration below depicts the uniform of an *Oberscharführer,* Allgemeine-SS; lower left, eight grades higher in rank, is an *Oberführer,* Allgemeine-SS. From the ordinary SS ranker up to the lofty heights of Himmler's own rank – *Reichsführer-SS* – there was a ladder of 17 grades of promotion. The top three (*Gruppenführer, Obergruppenführer,* and *Oberst-Gruppenführer*) soon came to rival the generals and admirals of the regular armed forces. The Allgemeine-SS (the regular SS) was distinct from the Waffen-SS (or SS armed forces, which fought alongside regular army units) – and it was the Allgemeine-SS which had the job of supervising Himmler's policy of racial extermination. The smaller illustrations on the right show SS posters: *top:* the SS crushing the 'Red Dragon'; *below:* Flemings, 'people of similar blood', are called to be good comrades in the common fight.

ERSATZKOMMANDO DER WAFFEN ⚡⚡
44, RUE DE LA LOI BRUXELLES

VOLKEN VAN GELIJKEN BLOEDE
STRIJDEN GEMEENSCHAPPELIJK
TEGEN DENZELFDEN VIJAND

VRIJWILLIGERS UIT DUITSCHLAND NEDERLAND VLAANDEREN
DENEMARKEN NOORWEGEN MELDEN ZICH AAN VOOR DE WAFFEN-⚡⚡

Deirdre Amsden

Armed help for the *Herrenvolk*

Left: SS *Sturmbannführer* Léon Degrelle, commander of the Walloon volunteers, salutes as SS General Felix Steiner is decorated by Hitler. *Below:* Four Russian brothers, all volunteers, sport their new German uniforms and death's-head badges

I SS
Panzer Division
'Liebstandarte'

II SS
Panzer Division
'Das Reich'

III SS
Panzer Division
'Totenkopf'

IV SS
Pz Gren Division
'Polizei Division'

V SS
Panzer Division
'Wiking'

VI SS
Mountain Division
'Nord'

VII SS
Vol Mnt Division
'Prinz Eugen'

VIII SS
Cavalry Division
'Florian Geyer'

IX SS
Panzer Division
'Hohenstaufen'

X SS
Panzer Division
'Frundsberg'

XI SS
Frw Pz Gr Div
'Nordlan I'

XII SS
Panzer Division
'Hitlerjugend'

XIII SS
Mountain Division
'Handschar'

XIV SS
Waffen Gren Division
'Galizische No I'

XV SS
Waffen Gren Division
'Latvian No I'

XVI SS
Pz Gren Division
'Reichsfuhrer SS'

XVII SS
Pz Gren Division
'Gotz von Berlichingen'

XVIII SS
Vol Pz Gren Division
'Horst Wessel'

XIX SS
Waffen Gren Division
'Latvian No II'

XX SS
Waffen Gren Division
'Estonian No I'

XXI Waffen
Geb Div der SS
'Skanderbeg'

XXII SS
Frw Kav Division
'Maria Theresa'

XXIII SS Vol Pz
Gren Division
'Nederland'

XXIV SS Waffen
Mountain Division
'Karstjager'

XXV SS
Waffen Gren Division
'Hungarian No II'

XXVI SS
Waffen Gren Div
'Hungarian No III'

XXVII SS
Vol Gren Division
'Flemish No I'

XXVIII SS
Vol Pz Gren Division
'Wallonie'

XXIX SS
Waffen Gren Division
'Italian No I'

XXX SS
Waffen Gren Division
'Russian No II'

XXXI SS
Frw Gren
Division

SS Frw
Gren Division
'Bohmen-Mahren'

XXXII SS
Vol Gren Division
'January 30'

XXXIII SS
Waf Gren Division
'Charlemagne'

XXXIV SS
Gren Division
'Landstorm Nederland'

XXXV SS
Pol Gren Division
'Polizei Division II'

XXXVI SS
Waffen Gren Division
'Dirlewanger'

XXXVII SS
Vol Cavalry Division
'Lutzow'

XXXVIII SS
Pz Gren Div
'Nibelungen'

THE
SCHUTZSTAFFEN
DIVISIONS

Badges of the 39 SS divisions

152

Emblems and Equipment of the Nazis and their supporters

1: First World War ex-serviceman's badge ('My Service'). **2:** Parabellum pistol. **3:** Baltic Cross (semi-official decoration for Germans who fought against the Bolsheviks on the Baltic front). **4:** Hitler Jugend belt buckle. **5:** Blood Order (given to those who took part in the Munich Putsch of 1923). **6:** Nazi Party badge. **7:** Early SS belt buckle. **8:** Mackensen commemorative clasp. **9:** Labour Corps (period between Hitler Youth and military training) belt buckle. **10:** Enamel plaque ('With us') fixed on houses, vehicles, etc, of party members. **11:** Lapel button (semi-official, worn by Germans who fought against Poles in Silesia in 1923). **12:** SS dagger ('My honour is faithfulness'). **13:** Dutch SS belt buckle. **14:** Lapel button commemorating SA rally in 1931

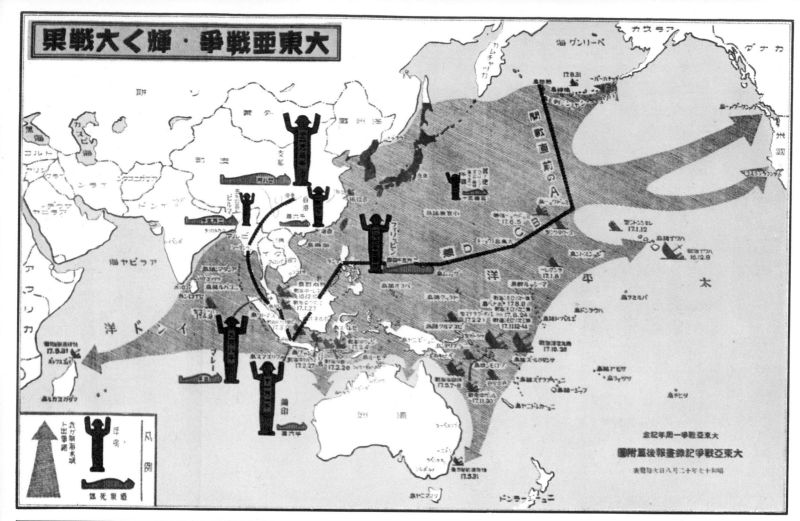

果戦大く輝・爭戦亜東大

(The School Weekly The **Primer** Edition) 大正四年六月四日第三種郵便物認可 第七十六卷第十一號 昭和十八年六月十四日發行 定價三錢

Vol. 76, No. 11 Tokyo, Mon., June 14, 1943 (Edited by N. Imai) Price 3 *sen.*

THE JAPANESE HAVE BIG PLANS

—from *The Daily Express, London.*

敵來襲英は對日反攻を頻りに呼びながら、未だに皇軍の南方占領地の一端に對してすら手を染め得ない。「對日反攻」を呼ぶのは「對日恐怖」を自ら慰める手段かも知れない。こゝに紹介した一篇に依つても、それが推し量られる。揭載紙はロンドンの"デイリ・エクスプレス"紙である。

① "Ever since the loss of Burma, I have been planning its re-occupation," said General Wevell. And ever since her conquest of Burma, Japan has been preparing, too.

big plan (尨大な意圖). **Ever since** (...以來絶えず). **loss** (喪失). **plan** (圖る). **re-occupation** (奪回). **General Wevell** [wi:vəl]. (英、印度軍司令官) **her conquest** (日本に依る征服). **be preparing** (戰備をとゝのへる)

② The inner circle in the map includes the area already occupied, bounded by the western borders of Burma.

inner circle (内側の圖). **include** (...を含む). **area** [ɛəriə] (範圍、地域). **already occupied** (すでに占領されたる). **bounded by~** (~に依り限られた). **border** (國境).

③ The outer circle represents the limit of Japan's future advance,

which includes the eastern part of India.... the circle strikes the coast in the region of Hyderabad and takes in Nepal in the north, chops through Tibet.

outer circle (外圖). **represent** (...を表はす). **limit** (限度). **future advance** (將來の進攻). **strike** (...に打當る). **region** (地域). **Hyderabad** (印度のインダス河に沿ふ都市). **take in~** (北は...を取り入れる). **Nepal** (ヒマラヤ山脈の中部). **chop through** (中斷する). **Tibet** (チベット).

④ It would be necessary for Japan to occupy Ceylon. In the south the circle touches the tip of northwestern Australia to include Darwin.

It would be **necessary for~to** (~が...することが必要となるだらう). **Ceylon** [silɔ́n] (セイロン島). **In the south** (南部は). **touch the tip** (...の端に達する). **to include Darwin** (ダーウキンを取圍んで).

記練事廈用題	● 第一次世界大戰の敗戰後ドイツは復興 (revival) を企圖して居た。 ● 今や日本の勢力は東亞全域を包括して居る。 ● 日本の今後の攻撃はその限度を知らぬ。それはワシントンの階落を以て多分止まるであらう。 ● 米國は日本の膨脹 (expansion) を力づくでも	even by force) 抑へようとした。その間日本も手を揑いては居なかつた。 America's offensive arms now reach the Aleutians in the north while striking the South Pacific in the south. Indeed they include the Eastern Hemisphere.

(The School Weekly The **Primer** Edition) 大正四年六月四日第三種郵便物認可 第七十六卷第十一號 昭和十八年七月五日發行 定價 3 錢

Vol. 76, No. 11 Tokyo, Mon., July 5, 1943 (Edited by N. Imai) Price 3 *sen.*

DEFENCE OF WAKE ISLAND

最近來の Wake Island (ウェーキ島) が、皇軍に占領された時の戰況を映畫化して Defence Of Wake Island と題してゐる。敗戰の事實はホンの一寸用ひて、米軍が如何に勇敢に戰したかを見せてゐる積りである、Jap などと憎しみのこもつた言葉を使つてゐるして、諷刺的だが且つ生る場面のタイトルの英文を紹介する。

① Waves of Japanese bombers sweep in over the sea, to bomb the island yard by yard. The island is bombed and shelled until it is one huge crater.

waves of bombers [báməz] (爆撃機の怒濤). **sweep in over~** (...の上空を席巻する). (cf. to sweep in (ただに込む)). **yard by yard** (點に點に、しらみつぶしに). *cf.* We proceeded **inch by inch.** (我等はジリジリと進んだ) They retreated **yard by yard** (被等は徐々に退いた). **is bombed and shelled** (爆撃され砲撃される). (cf. shell (砲撃、爆撃を打ち込む) **huge crater** (巨大な噴火口).

② The island's last plane reports that a big enemy fleet is approaching and soon afterwards the Japs begin their landing attempt.

report (報ず). **fleet** (艦隊). **approach** (接近する). **soon afterwards** (次で間もなく). **landing** (上陸). **attempt** (企て、行動).

③ The Marines cut them down with machine-guns fire and hand grenades. But there are too many Japs and too few Marines. The invader establish a beach-head.

Marine [mərin] (海兵). **machine-gun fire** (機關銃火). **hand grenades** [grineidz] (手榴彈). **Jap** (Japanese の蔑稱). **invader** (侵略者). **establish beach-head** (海岸線を確立する(海岸の一角を確保すること)).

④ At Pearl Harbour Radio Station an officer is handed a message from the Commander of the island: "The enemy has landed. The issue is still in doubt." Then there is silence.

Pearl Harbour (眞珠灣). **Radio Station** (無線局). **officer** (士官). **hand** (手交する). **message** (通牒). **Commander** (司令官). **issue** [iʃju:] (結末). **in doubt** (不明なり). **there in silence** (音信絶ゆ).

記事應用練習課題	● 我が兵は陣地 (position) の一なだれを打つて侵入した。 ● 船は連續爆撃されてその全貌 (whole shape) を一變した。 ● わが守備兵は手榴彈を以て、次で爆彈を投じて閉つた。 ● 敵軍は島の三方から上陸を企て ● "Those that are left of us are going to attack the invaders as a whole." The report said, "we shall fight to the last man." Then there was silence.

154

THE WAR THROUGH JAPANESE EYES

Until the beginning of 1943, the war had little effect on the everyday life of the Japanese civilian, except on those families with sons in the forces. Saturated by glowing reports of startlingly easy victories and cushioned by propaganda from news of the first setbacks, the Japanese public felt that the war was a successful gamble. **Below:** Four examples of a news sheet for schools which emphasised Japan's victories and denigrated the Allies. The right-hand sheet features the Japanese-supported Indian nationalist leader Subhas Chandra Bose, whom the Japanese hoped would become the leader of a puppet Indian government. Much Japanese propaganda was designed to appeal to the latent nationalism of the Asian races against the Western colonial powers. **Left:** A Japanese map printed during the period of expansion. Compared with the map on page 1386, it overemphasises the size of Japanese forces in the south, and exaggerates the extent of Japanese strikes against the Allies. **Right:** Part of a leaflet 'deifying' the men lost at Pearl Harbor: one facet of the modern Samurai code which governed Japan's attitude towards the war, and inspired her troops to such incredible feats of bravery, endurance, and savagery

Nine Heroes' Memories Will Live Forever

横山正治少佐　　古野繁實少佐　　　　　　　佐々木直吉特務少尉　上田定兵曹長

廣尾彰大尉　　横山薫範特務少尉　　岩佐直治中佐　　　片山義雄兵曹長　稲垣清兵曹長

The superhuman work performed by the Special Attack Flotilla at Pearl Harbor at the outset of the war, their matchless devotion to duties, and their utter disregard of life or death clearly entitle them to be classed as gods.

They gave the very best they had in them and their own lives as well for the task to which they had set their hearts and souls. None of the nine has come back. Their mortal remains will probably lie embedded forever at the bottom of Pearl Harbor.

(The ABC Weekly) 大正四年二月六日第三種郵便認可　第七十四卷第十一號　每月十七日二回發行　定價三錢

THE ABC WEEKLY

Vol. 74 No. 11 Tokyo, Mon., Nov. 16, 1942. (Edited by N. Imai) Price 3 sen.

We have a new **Ministry**.

It is the **Greater East Asia** Ministry.

Mr. Kazuo Aoki is the **Minister** of the new Ministry.

*

Here you see some American **airmen**.

They are the **crew** of the American planes which **raided** Japan on April 18.

They have been **punished with heavy penalties.**

The crew of any aircraft raiding Japan will be punished **with death.**

We have a ~ (......が出来た). new ministry (新しい官省). [cf. minister (大臣); ministry (內閣、官廳)].

Greater East Asia Ministry (grèitə ìːst éiʃə ministri) (大東亜省).

*

Here you see~ (ここに......が居る). Américan (米國の). airmen (飛行士). crew (乘員). plane=airplane (飛行機). ráided (襲んだ). April (四月). heavy pénalty (重き罰則). aircraft (航空機). ráiding Japan (日本を犯す). be púnished (罰せられる). with death (死罰

を賦する).
cf. { to punish with death (死刑に處す).
{ to escape with life (生命を全うす).

◇ 記事應用練習題 ◇

❶ 大東亜大區の青木氏は長野縣の出身である (come from~).
❷ 如何なる敵も日本を犯して成功したことはない (to raid successfully).
❸ 組組は皆んと共に沈んだ.
❹ この徒 (law) を破つた者は重く罰せられます.
❺ No penalty, even death itself is enough for those who have sold their own country.

(The School Weekly The Primer Edition) 大正四年六月四日第三種郵便認可　昭和十六年第十五號　每月十七日二回發行　定價三錢

THE SCHOOL WEEKLY THE PRIMER EDITION

Vol. 76, No. 15. Tokyo, Mon., July 12, 1943 (Edited by N. Imai) Price 3 sen.

SUBHAS CHANDRA BOSE

Subhas Chandra Bose, famous Indian leader in the move for independence from Britain has appeared in Tokyo. He will exhaust all means to help expel Anglo-Saxon influences from India.

Subhas Chandra Bose [súːbas tʃǽndrə bouz]. fámous (有名な). leader (指導者). move for~ (......運動) [cf. to start a move (運動を起す)]. Indepéndence (獨立). has appéared (現はれた). exhaust [igzɔ́ːst] (盡す). all means (萬策). to help expel=to help to expel (驅逐を促す, 追出す様うに). Anglo-Saxon influences (英米の勢力).

Whites-Negroes Battle :—Serious riots between Whites and Negroes broke out in Detroit, U.S. 23 have been killed and 700 seriously injured in the fighting.

Students of Peers' School :—Eighteen students in the first year class of the Higher School Division of the Peers' School have enrolled in the Student Aviation Corps.

Preparedness

Mother : "I hope you didn't take a second helping of cake at the party, son ?"

Son : "No, Ma, I took two pieces the first time."
— Copper's Weekly.

Whites-Negroes Battle
sérious [síːriəs] (由々しき). riot [ráiət] (騷動). Whites (白人). Négroes (黒人). broke out (突發した). Detroit (U.S. Michigan 州の一都市). be sériously ínjured [indʒəd] (重傷を負ふ). in the fighting (爭闘の結果).

Students of Peers' School
students in the first class (一年生). Higher School Division (高等科). Peers' School (學習院). have enrólled (入隊した). Aviátion Corps [eiviéiʃən kɔː] (航空隊).

Preparedness
Preparedness [pripéədnis] (用意周到). second helping (おかはり). cf.[I helped myself to the cake (私は勝手に菓子を取つて食べた). at the party (御客の席で). Ma=Mother. two pieces (二片). the first time (最初に).

Highest Honor Granted

His Majesty the Emperor was gracious enough to confer the title of Fleet-Admiral on Admiral Nagano and that of Field-Marshal on General Terauchi and General Sugiyama.

His Majesty the Emperor (天皇陛下). was gracious enough to~ (廣くも......し給へり). confer on~ (......に授ける). title (稱號). Fleet-Admiral (海軍元帥). that of (......の稱號). Field Marshal (陸軍元帥の稱號). Admiral (海軍大将). General (陸軍大将).

今學期は今號を以つて發行を終り第二學期は九月六日第一號を發行す.

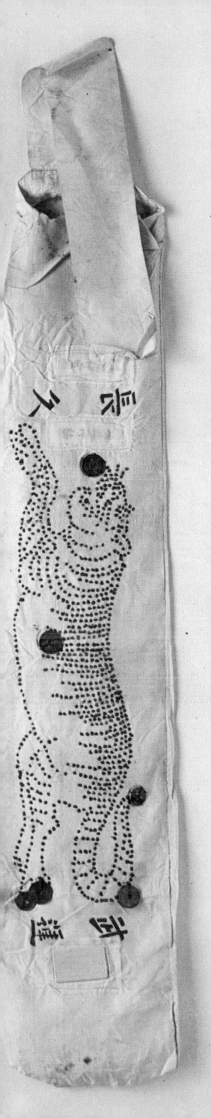

Relics of Japan's War Cult

The Japanese war cult was a concept difficult for the western soldier to understand, for only to the Japanese soldier was battle an act of worship to his Emperor and death in battle sacramental. The Japanese army was a strange blend of old and new: the samurai sword was as vital to an officer in battle as was his machine-pistol. And during the approach to battle, fanatical adherence to the Bushido code of military honour inflamed all ranks, invoking feats of tenacity and endurance — as well as futile sacrifice — which will probably remain unique in the annals of war

Far left: A Japanese 'Rising Sun' battle flag, inscribed with Shinto prayers. These flags were among the trophies most sought after by Allied souvenir-hunters

Centre: The *senninbari,* a soldier's personal 'belt of a thousand stitches', which would be made for him by his family to be worn into battle. Worn around the waist under the uniform, it was supposed to confer luck, courage — and immunity from enemy fire

Left: A wound tag, used to locate the site of an injury. The Japanese army probably had the worst medical facilities of the fighting powers, and captured medical equipment was highly prized

Below: Japanese soldiers were often issued with packs of field postcards, usually produced in two different styles. The dashing battle scene — with appropriate war-cries — is illustrated here, but the other style typified another side of Japanese life: serene studies of chrysanthemum blooms, birds perching on branches, misty views of mountains, lanterns at dusk

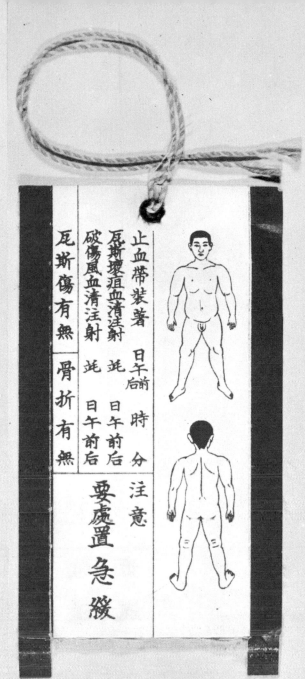

The final ignominy—under the watchful eyes of Indian soldiers, Japanese officers surrender their swords

GV R1

HE whom this scroll commemorates was numbered among those who, at the call of King and Country, left all that was dear to them, endured hardness, faced danger, and finally passed out of the sight of men by the path of duty and self-sacrifice, giving up their own lives that others might live in freedom. Let those who come after see to it that his name be not forgotten.

Above: To the grieving relatives of British soldiers killed in the First World War, the King sent this commemorative scroll.